The LOST ART of being a Lady

THIS IS A PRION BOOK

This edition published in 2015 by Prion
An imprint of the Carlton Publishing Group
20 Mortimer Street
London W1T 3JW

First published in 2006 as *How to Boil a Flamingo*

Introduction and selected text copyright © Alison Rattle, Allison Vale 2006
Design copyright © Carlton Publishing Group 2006
Illustrations copyright © Merrily Harpur 2006

A catalogue record for this book is available from the British Library.

ISBN: 978-1-85375-925-3

Printed and bound in Dubai

The LOST ART of being a Lady

A Victorian Self-help Guide for MODERN WOMEN

Allison Vale & Alison Rattle

PRION

To my loveliest virtuosities: Thomas and Louisa

A.V.

For my two little ladies and my fine young gentleman:
Daisy, Ella and Riley

A.R.

'A woman, especially if she has the misfortune of knowing anything, should conceal it as well as she can.'

Jane Austen

Contents

Introduction

A woman is born with a keen and ready wit; she has a natural capacity for seeing and comprehending the way of things. 'Tis true, she may not be schooled or tutored in the same manner as her brother, but this alone will not inhibit that sense and reason with which she will come to steer and influence the course taken by her husband in all things. A good marriage, secured in respect of a young lady's virtuous ways and gracious living, will bestow upon her all its inherent status and power. Day by day, it is the gentleman who carries the practical burdens of business and politics; unquestionably, it is his *wife* who informs his very conscience.

In this way, society has come to be *noiselessly directed* by the *wives* that adorn the parlours of their men. It is her *sensibility* that gains a woman access, little by little, to the cerebral world of her husband. In time, as she perfects the art of listening, his trust in her will grow; he will soon come to regard it as a relief, indeed, to sit with her and unburden his mind in matters of business, finance and politics. How small a step is it then for the wife to begin to *steer the course of his mind*? With the well-timed question and the shrewd inquiry, a wife can influence her husband's decisions and manipulate his actions in all his most weighty and troublesome concerns.

Think not, then, that the world of etiquette, or the private toilet of a lady, is but an inconsequential triviality. By forming a character based on the very best of models, a gentlewoman may conduct herself as if she were a well-bred and refined lady in the very *highest* sense. Be not deceived by the trifling semblance of respectable pastimes, or acceptable superstitions, for herein lies the key to your successful passage to prominence in all things.

It can happen that a woman of genteel aspirations has, for some reason (whether of birth or pecuniary disadvantage), been precluded from expert tutorage in the ways of a lady. Furthermore, the *correct* education of the female mind has, of late, been everywhere neglected. We feel it is our duty, therefore, to offer you in the pages that follow the very best guidance to assist in the stimulation and direction of your feminine wit and character. This work has been undertaken by us, at the cost of much time and fiscal discomfort, for your peculiar convenience and advancement. We hope our earnest efforts in these matters will promote the growth of the loftiest and holiest traits of heart and mind, fitting you for the fulfilment of the highest of earthly missions: marriage. Should our miscellany prove to benefit but *one* unschooled mind, then we will be *ravished* with contentment! Indeed, none could be more abundantly rewarded.

A word of caution before proceeding: sensibility, that most indispensable of feminine qualities, can only be *perfected* by studious practice; it cannot be created. Where a raw, unhoned quantity of this inherent virtue is not first in existence, it can never be entirely learned nor artificially adopted. In such cases, it were better that a woman desist in her efforts to progress, and content herself instead with that lesser status that God, in His Wisdom, has ordained for her. A lady must first be *born*, before she can perfect the craft.

How to be Presented at Court

'ON THE DAY ITSELF YOU WILL NEED A STEADY NERVE, AND
THE PATIENCE OF THE SAINTS! ... PRAY FOR COMPOSURE,
GOOD DEPORTMENT AND A STEADY FOOTING!'

For any young lady born into a good family nothing can be
the source of more eager anticipation than the occasion
of her presentation at Court. For it is this moment, in the
presence of Their Most Gracious Majesties, that trumpets
the commencement of a life of balls, gay festivities and, most
exhilarating of all, marriage negotiations. There seems little
cause to elaborate upon who should be eligible for such an
event; however, for the benefit of our varied readership, we
shall endeavour to enlighten. None but those of the highest
possible moral calibre should be presented: the divorcee and
the actress, along with any who have committed adultery,
are barred. Welcomed are all ladies of noble paternity, naturally, along with daughters of the noble professions: the
barrister, the physician, the officer, the clergyman. The
general practitioner, the businessman, or the solicitor need
not contemplate presenting their womenfolk.

There are many preparations that will need to occupy the several weeks before the ceremony. See to it that you secure an excellent mantua maker. Court dress has its own dictates and does not adhere to any ordinary principles of fashion. Formal evening wear simply will not do! The mantua gown, with its full skirts and broad panniers, is *de rigueur*. It matters not that this has been outmoded in general society for many a decade. It is not outmoded at Court!

Your bodice must be short in the sleeve and your neckline plunging so that your feminine charms are held proudly aloft. (This last, a necessity by Royal decree: at the King's behest, the only exceptions are to be at the written application of a respected physician insisting that such an exposure of the *décolletage* would be detrimental to a lady's person or well-being.)

One must wear white, though delicate detailing in the lightest shades is entirely becoming. Hence, with the simplest of adaptations, your court mantua and your wedding gown can be one and the same. See that your mantua maker creates two bodices to accompany the skirt: one with the daintiest of sleeves and a falling neckline befitting your day at Court, the other more appropriate for your wedding. If you are to be conspicuously elegant, spare no expense in the creation of your costume. Embroidered displays in silver and gold threads are most becoming. Your headpiece, too, will be of weighty significance. Her Majesty, Queen Charlotte, requests that a single, elegant ostrich feather be fixed to your high, veiled headdress.

Whilst most seemly, they are notoriously challenging to wear, particularly at the moment of the curtsey. See that yours is thoroughly fastened! Finally, your train is essential. At 10 feet in length, it will require that you rehearse well before the event: walking in graciously is one thing; walking out, without turning your back on Their Majesties, is quite another! A length of linen pinned to your shoulders will act as a most useful mock-train in which you may perfect the art.

Every lady will require a sponsor. This is most often her mother, but any female relative already at Court will do. For those unfortunates who have no surviving lady relative at Court, there are those who will act as sponsor, but only in exchange for a fee. It goes without saying that any lady should look to her sponsor's reputation beforehand, seeking an unyielding respectability.

Your final preparation will be in the mastering of the Royal curtsey. For many, this will require expert tuition for which there are many respectable tutors from whom you may choose. The curtsey is exacting, involving a deep drop, so that the knee skims the surface of the floor, where it remains for a long moment, before you rise to your feet with consummate control. In your deportment too, you must appear regal (if only to ensure the safe-keeping of your headdress!).

On the day itself you will need a steady nerve, and the patience of the saints! Have your coachman wait in front of St James's Palace until you are beckoned within. Be warned: the wait can be considerable! Within the doors of the Palace you will be placed in accordance with your father's rank, and then here, too, you will have a lengthy wait. Use your time wisely: pray for composure, good deportment and a steady footing! Finally, your moment will have arrived. The Lord Chamberlain, having been presented with your card, will announce you. The great doors of St James's Hall will open, whereupon you will face a vast room, at the far end of which sit Their Majesties and numerous attendants. A footman will have arranged your train so that it is flawless. Remember your training: glide across the room as if on air! Curtsey graciously and kiss the Royal hand. If your father be of high nobility, a Duke or an Earl, the Royal kiss will be bestowed upon your forehead. Thereafter, you should rise to your feet and repeat the curtsey for any other noble attendants.

With a final bow to Their Majesties, gather up your train – if needs be with the assistance of a footman. May your steps out be purposeful, sound and sure! Alas, the poor misfortunate who loses her footing on her exit, to the cost of her train, her headdress and her happy future!

THE LONG TRADITION OF THE PRESENTATION OF YOUNG LADIES AT COURT, WHICH VARIED LITTLE OVER CENTURIES, BASED HERE ON THE COURT FASHIONS OF KING GEORGE III AND QUEEN CHARLOTTE

How to Best Employ Your Calling Card

'ENSURE THAT YOUR CARD IS NEITHER TOO PLAIN NOR
TOO OSTENTATIOUS. YOUR NAME SHOULD BE PRINTED IN
SUFFICIENTLY LARGE TYPE SO AS TO MAKE IT CLEARLY
LEGIBLE WITHOUT APPEARING BOISTEROUS.'

A lady should always carry her card in sufficient
numbers if she is to persist in giving it out abroad that
she is still in society. Firstly, ensure that your card is
neither too plain nor too ostentatious. Your name should
be printed in sufficiently large a type so as to make it
clearly legible without appearing boisterous. (The
current fashion in some quarters for miniature print can
only have the effect of making you appear trivial and
prone to whimsy – to be avoided, then, at all costs.) You
may add your address and, if you have an 'At Home' day,
this can also be printed. If you are planning to make calls
accompanied by your sons or daughters, their names
should also be printed on your cards.

A married lady must, of course, also carry with her the
card of her husband, and should carry these in a quantity

double in size to her own. Each card of your own that you leave must be accompanied by two of your husband's: one for the hostess, the other for the gentleman of the house.

A calling card left at the beginning of the season announces your arrival to everyone in society upon whom you are desirous to call. Bear in mind that, as a general rule, it will not be possible for anyone to call upon an acquaintance more frequently than once in a season in so large a city as London or Bath.

Gentlemen may turn down a corner of their card if they are delivering it in person: whilst it is inappropriate for a lady to do so, a turned-down card can be a useful way of conveying that you intend to call upon all those currently residing in the house. (Etiquette would be far better served, however, if you left a card for each one.)

See that you restrict your calls to the hours of 3 o'clock until 6 o'clock though they are known by all as 'morning' calls, this is simply a manner of speaking. It would be ruinous to assume one must therefore arrive before mid-afternoon. Any earlier and you will impair a lady's fulfilling all those avocations that occupy her hours before lunch. We are aware that in the country some are wont to persist in the odious habit of calling before noon! See that you are never guilty of such an imposition in the city. And any time beyond 6 o'clock, in London in particular, will infringe upon your hostess's evening drive.

Your visits should, at most, be 20 minutes in length, no matter how animated the conversation may prove to be during that time. Greet civilly any stranger you meet in the hostess's drawing room during your call; thereafter you are under no obligation to offer them any recognition should you encounter them – for instance, whilst promenading. Should a new visitor be admitted whilst you are seated, you should make your goodbyes and leave only moments later unless you are invited to remain.

Distinctions must be made between calls of differing purposes. A formal call, such as in response to an invitation to a wedding reception or dinner party, should be made in most instances within a week of receiving such an invitation. If you are making calls to announce your recent arrival in a new town or city, you should do so at your very earliest opportunity. In this instance, it is better to remain in your carriage and have your servant deliver the card. In any case, refrain from inquiring whether the lady of the house is at home on a first visit. Residents will make the first call in person to the newcomer. Following a ceremonial event, such as a wedding or a ball, you should call to leave your card a day or two later. In this instance it will suffice to leave your card without requesting admittance. Any call, or calling card, of which you are in receipt, should be returned in kind within 10 days.

Finally, you should inform yourself of the appropriate form in which to convey information on your card. Never simply write 'accept' or 'regret' on a card in response to an invitation; this is most impertinent. However, there are some messages it is perfectly seemly to convey in brief on your card, so long as you do so in the appropriate manner. The following contractions bear messages succinctly and act as a good indication of your social attentiveness:

* *pf* (*pour féliciter*) will adequately express your congratulations.
* *pr* (*pour remercier*) offers your thanks for any act of kindness.
* *pc* (*pour condoléances*) will suffice following a bereavement for a week after the event.
* *pfNA* (*pour féliciter Nouvel An*) extends your wishes for a Happy New Year when calling on New Year's Day.
* *ppc* (*pour prendre congé*) informs the household that you and your family will be leaving the area.
* *pp* (*pour présenter*) announces your desire to be introduced to the hostess.

ADAPTED FROM ORIGINAL ADVICE IN *A HANDBOOK OF ETIQUETTE FOR LADIES AND GENTLEMEN*, JAMES HOGG & SONS, LONDON, 1859

How to Wear a Hobble Garter

'A LADY MUST BE ON HER GUARD AT ALL TIMES NOT TO TAKE TOO LARGE A STRIDE WHEN HURRYING TO A PRESSING ENGAGEMENT OR ATTEMPTING TO CLIMB A STAIR, LEST THE SEAMS OF HER SKIRT BE RIPPED SHAMEFULLY OPEN.'

In matters of high fashion a lady must prove resolute, adopting the most remarkable features of feminine toilet whilst closing her ears to denouncements which may rain down from pulpits or from out of the mouths of eminent physicians. If fashion dictates the wearing of a hobble garter (that ingenious device designed to assist in the wearing of a hobble skirt), then a lady must make haste to introduce one at once to her wardrobe.

A hobble skirt should drape softly around the hips and taper very narrowly down towards the ankles. It may be fashioned from the most discreet and plainest of fabrics for everyday wear, or from the finest quality silks and satins for evening soirées and days at the races. A delightful addition, which resembles an ornate lampshade and is wired to keep its shape, may be hung from the waist to give a most fashionable silhouette. It must be noted that the tighter and narrower the hem of the hobble skirt, the more modish it will appear.

A narrow hemline confines the wearer to taking the most mincing of steps, which appear most refined and feminine, but a lady must be on her guard at all times not to take too large a stride when hurrying to a pressing engagement or when attempting to climb a stair, lest the seams of her skirt be ripped shamefully open. Let all fears on this matter be put to rest, for the hobble garter has been designed to put paid to this disarming and discomforting plight. This truly clever contraption is a veritable miracle of engineering, consisting of two garters held together by a strip of elastic some two to three inches long. The garters are slipped on to your silk-covered calves, then concealed by the length of your hobble skirt. They are wholly effective in preventing you from taking steps of more than the required two to three inches and thus succeed in keeping your hobble skirt intact!

When wearing a hobble skirt and garter, you will look and feel very like a concubine from an Oriental harem, and you must be careful to arrange your everyday movements accordingly. Your daily constitutionals must not be of too great a distance and you must take care not to imbibe too much in the way of fluids lest you are caught unawares by needs of a personal nature.

There may be women all around you desperately

protesting against the fettering of the female form and drawing attention to themselves in their bid to win women's suffrage. Be assured that the hobble garter will heighten your sense of elegance and self-possession, present you as the very epitome of fashion, and will certainly win you much admiration from the opposite sex; all this beyond anything that may be accomplished by chaining oneself to an iron railing.

BASED ON EARLY EDWARDIAN LADIES' FASHION. THE HOBBLE SKIRT WAS DESIGNED BY PAUL POIRET IN 1910

How to Boil a Flamingo

'IT IS THE DUTY OF ANY HOSTESS TO PROVIDE A MEMORABLE
DINING EXPERIENCE, AND THIS DISH, IF COOKED WITH CARE,
WILL SATISFY EVEN THE MOST CHALLENGING OF GUESTS.'

When entertaining guests one must always endeavour to impress them with the richness and comfort of one's dining-room. A dinner party should be as elegant an affair as possible with a lavishly appointed table laid out with your best and most costly china.

As you will have spent much time deliberating over the phrasing of your invitations, the mix of guests and the décor and arrangement of your dining-room, it follows that your menu should be of the highest quality and exceedingly agreeable. A brace of roasted partridges is most acceptable when dining *en famille*, but a dish which speaks eloquently of your superior taste and flair (and of the depths of your husband's pockets) is more suitable when striving to uphold a much envied position as society's most fashionable hostess.

How to Boil a Flamingo

It is the duty of any hostess to provide a memorable dining experience, and this dish, if cooked with care, will satisfy even the most challenging of guests.

1. Secure a flamingo and relieve it of feathers.

2. Remove any undesirable parts of the bird that you do not wish to consume, such as innards, head, feet etc. (These offcuts need not go to waste; a competent cook can turn them into the tastiest of stocks.)

3. Wash the flamingo thoroughly and place in a large pan of water along with aniseed, vinegar and a pinch of seasoning.

4. Bring to the boil and simmer quietly for an hour. The scent of aniseed released at this juncture is most delectable to inhale.

5. At this point may be added some roughly chopped leeks, fresh coriander and a few spoons of port wine into the pan. Cover with a lid and let cook for a further 20 minutes.

6. Make use of a pestle and mortar to crush together some black peppercorns, cumin seeds, coriander seeds, laser root, fresh rue and mint. Add some vinegar to bind the mixture into a paste.

7. Remove the now-cooked flamingo from the pan and add your paste and some dates to the cooking mixture. Boil rapidly to reduce, adding some flour if necessary to thicken the sauce.

8. Send your flamingo to the table garnished in the most flamboyant manner possible and serve slices to your guests with the date sauce poured on top.

If you have difficulty procuring a flamingo, then we have it on good authority that a half dozen parrots cooked in the same manner can result in just as impressive a dish.

ADAPTED FROM A LATE MEDIEVAL FRENCH COOK BOOK

How to Create Artistic Dimples

'NOTHING SPEAKS OF INNOCENCE AND VIRTUE MORE THAN
THE NATURAL INDENTATIONS OF CHILDHOOD, LINGERING
LONG INTO WOMANHOOD ... HOW LAMENTABLE, THEN, IS
THE MORNING WHEN A LADY GAZES FIRST UPON THE GLASS
AND SHRINKS BACK IN DISMAY AT THE SIGHT OF HER
FADING FACIAL FISSURE?'

How envied by all young ladies is she who displays a brace of natural dimples upon a pink-and-white complexion! For nothing speaks of innocence and virtue more than the natural indentations of childhood, lingering long into womanhood. No other feature can match the dimple in its ability to sing of the sweet purity that exists in the heart. What young gentleman can resist its charm? One glance at the blushed cheek framing such a tiny treasure and he is surely smitten, as if Cupid himself has drawn his bow. However daintily footed, however prettily coiffed, nothing can surpass the beauty of the dimple, divine in its simplicity.

How lamentable, then, is the morning when a lady

gazes first upon the glass and shrinks back in dismay at the sight of her fading facial fissure. How she must mourn her waning youth, bemoan her diminishing beauty, fear for her chances of ever acquiring a beau! No amount of cream, potion or balsam has hitherto proved efficacious in the least at halting the degeneration of the dimple. No pounding, probing or pummelling has deepened that collapsing pit. Alas, 'tis a moment fit for mourning!

Along with the matter of durability, Mother Nature is not always so judicious in the distribution of these most highly-prized niches. She has not always seen fit to position a dimple in the most apt location. How many of us have winced at the sight of a chin, dimpled ever so slightly off-centre, with the resultant effect that the chin is rendered quite misshapen? Or else recoiled from the dimpled cheek, quite ruined by the imbalance of that on its opposite number? In such instances are Nature's dimples rendered quite worthless. How much better would it be, if one could select the exact location of one's dimple, and furthermore ensure its longevity?

With some elation, we now proclaim knowledge of the precise process with which this silent suffering may be alleviated. For the genius mind of one Herr Martin Goetze, resident of Berlin, in the kingdom of Prussia, has borne offspring that will come to a young lady's rescue as sure as St George when he slew the dragon. His patented device not only *nurtures* the existing dimple on the human body, but will go so far as to create one, *where one is not previously in existence*!

Goetze's scientific experimentation has revealed to him that it is necessary to first prepare the area of flesh surrounding the proposed site of the dimple. Massaging the tissue is the most effective method of preparation, and thus his device incorporates both a massage pearl and a massage cylinder, braced together in the fashion of a compass. For additional comfort the whole has been rendered adjustable to any position by means of a tele-scopic arm. Great care must be taken in the cellular preparation, for herein lies the key to success. The massage pearl, working in conjunction with the cylinder, communicates the desire for malleability to the flesh beneath the skin. Both the pearl and the cylinder can be constructed out of ivory or marble (though should a lady be desirous of planting a dimple in a more sensitive spot, she will find Indian rubber a more forgiving substance).

Once the skin has been made suitably pliable, you are ready to create your dimple, or enhance your existing one. Simply place the pearl in the precise spot upon your face, or area of the body with which you are concerned, holding it firm as you go. Next, position the cylinder and the arm correctly, and then begin the process of rotating the brace, which will have the effect of pushing the pearl into your skin, so as to create the dimple. The mechanism of the device is simplicity itself, and Herr Goetze assures all that its efficacy is quite unrivalled.

How to Create Artistic Dimples

The results will delight and astound you, though a word of caution may be in order, for so agreeable are the results that the process can be quite compulsive. We know of one or two ladies who have become so entranced by the production of dimples about their person that they are left pervasively pitted, which is not at all pleasing to the eye. Moderation, as in all things, is to be strictly observed.

INSPIRED BY MARTIN GOETZE'S, 'DEVICE FOR PRODUCING DIMPLES', PATENTED 19 MAY 1896

How to Attract the Attention of the Object of Your Affection

'THE MOST IMPORTANT QUALITY A WOMAN SHOULD EXHIBIT IN THE COMPANY OF MEN IS THE ABILITY TO BLUSH; WHEN SHE HAS LOST THIS, SHE LOSES HER MOST PREVAILING ALLURE.'

Courtship is, by its very nature, troublesome. It is made all the more so, given that it occurs at the very earliest moments of adulthood, when a young lady has but a fragile clutch on the world, and yet her passions, though still immature, are most fired up. Would that every young lady found herself in possession of so principled a spirit as would render her incapable of dishonesty, whilst maintaining a prudence so keen as to defend her against being misled!

You may be assured that foremost among feminine advantages is that humble diffidence and elusive reserve that avoids the public eye and is left ill at ease by appreciative glances. The most important quality a woman should exhibit in the company of men is the ability to blush; when she has lost this, she loses her most prevailing allure.

How to Attract the Attention of the Object of Your Affection

The modesty we urge you to maintain will make you essentially *silent in large gatherings*. But be sure that your hush does not exclude you from participation: show in your countenance and expression that *silence* does not signify *dullness*. When addressed by a gentleman of higher rank, be sure to sustain a remote familiarity, such as would not betray the flurry of your heart nor make visible what eager preference you may feel for said gentleman. You will thereby avoid puffing his sense of vanity, should he feel he has granted you a favour with his attention.

In male company it is of the utmost priority that you on no account display your wit, nor even so much good sense. If you possess these qualities, guard them closely: they can only make you enemies. Men will see a keen wit in a woman as most threatening and will assume you seek to assert your superiority over any assembled company. Most men will turn a malevolent eye on any woman of learning. See that you keep your cultivated opinions a clandestine trait, even from the most genius of men. Indeed, in conversation there is much to be gained from attentive listening. More men's hearts have been melted by persuasive *hearing* than talking.

No lady seeking to attract a gentleman's attentions should see fit to indulge in the current fashion for indecorous and luxuriant eating. Such coarseness is evident in the conduct of certain men, and is a contemptible trait. On no account must *ladies* of rank indulge, for to do so would be abhorrent. When eating in company, exhibit the same modesty and restraint that you do in every other aspect of your public countenance.

There is no merit to be gained in thrusting oneself into the eyes of a man who has attracted your attentions. The ball, or other public gathering, is no place to gain anything but a reputation for vanities. Moreover, conversing as freely with men as men do with each other, displaying all your charms in the process, will never persuade an honourable man to part with his heart. Instead, seek out the quiet company of men with whom you can enjoy easy and agreeable conversation; the surest way to develop a mutual admiration and uncover common predilections and sensibilities.

Any woman will instinctively shun the company of a lightweight man who will indulge a lady's attention simply to satisfy his own coquettish vanity. Thankfully, such a man is rare indeed as gentlemen of honour are too often preoccupied with matters of business to trouble themselves with winning a lady's affections; that which they know is already wholly within their influence. Similarly, refrain from indulging the attentions of a man whom you have no desire to marry simply to invest in your own vanity.

ADAPTED FROM *A FATHER'S LEGACY TO HIS DAUGHTERS*
BY DR GREGORY OF EDINBURGH, 1774

How to Employ the Formidable Weapon of Coquetry

'A FAN BECOMES A LADY AS MUCH AS A SWORD BECOMES
A GENTLEMAN AND YOU SHOULD STRIVE TO BECOME THE
MISTRESS OF YOUR WEAPON.'

The fan is, without doubt, an indispensable addition to any lady's toilet. It is a necessity beyond all considerations of fashion or style, and a lady *sans* fan is indeed a lady *sans* grace. If the air around you should smell less than sweet, and a foul odour assault your timorous nostrils, then it is only right that you should possess the means to waft the stink away with a flick of your wrist and present a more pleasing fragrance to yourself. When suffering from a delicacy of constitution, or when troubled with the vapours, what could be more reviving than a fluttering of cooling air to assist the breath? A fan is much used in summer to keep away the heat of the sun and to shield a delicate complexion from its savage rays; it is also much in use during the winter months to keep away the heat of the fires, which impart a red ugliness to the most porcelain of skins.

A lady may acquire an extraordinary passion for fans which will afford her the greatest of pleasures. Your passion should be aired abroad so as to reach the ears of your suitors, that they may know which gift is most likely to soften your heart. The most desirable of fans are wondrously elaborate and costly, carved from fragrant woods or fashioned in ivory, gold, silver or tortoiseshell and garnished with rubies or diamonds. You may find particular delight in the beauty of ostrich feathers; a lady looks unusually becoming when framed by such rich-ness. The leaves of your fan may be of paper, parchment, silk or the softest 'swan skin', and the opening of your fan should please all spectators when they look upon an agreeable scene of garlands, landscapes and all manner of birds and beasts executed by the most skilful of painters. Douse your fan from time to time with your favourite perfume so as always to leave behind a trace of your presence.

A fan becomes a lady as much as a sword becomes a gentleman and you should strive to become the mistress of your weapon: skilful in its handling and motions, and fluent in its language. There are many ways to unfurl your fan which require practice to perfect the little flirts and graceful vibrations. A lady is truly accomplished in her art if she can discharge her fan with a crack that may be heard at the far end of a room. This talent is most useful to advertise your entrance, or indeed to demonstrate your impatience and displeasure.

It is in the fluttering of a fan that a lady needs to employ her best efforts. You may learn the merry flutter, the angry flutter, the amorous flutter, the modest flutter; indeed, any person within wind of your fan should be capable of discerning your mood from the merest twitch of your wrist. A lady who executes her fan with flair may employ her cleverness to entrance or repel all gentlemen who approach her. Indeed, she need not utter a single word, or risk a blemish on her character for her thoughts to be understood. We lay down the most commonly used messages to be conveyed in the manner indicated.

* A resting of the fan on the right cheek: No.
* A resting of the fan on the left cheek: Yes.
* A fan placed close to the heart: You have won my love.
* To flutter the fan threateningly: I cannot tolerate your impudence!
* To fan languorously: I am already wed.

How to Employ the Formidable Weapon of Coquetry

* To fan quickly: I am engaged to be wed.
* To hold the fan in the left hand and place in front of the face: I wish to be acquainted with you.
* To hold the fan in the right hand and place in front of the face: It would please me if you were to follow me.
* To draw the fan across the eyes: I am sorry.
* To draw the fan across the hand: I find you utterly distasteful.
* To draw the fan across the cheek: I love you.
* To twirl the fan in the right hand: My heart belongs to another.
* To twirl the fan in the left hand: Be careful – all eyes are upon us!
* Presenting a shut fan: Do you have feelings for me?
* Placing the fan handle to the lips: I am desirous of your kisses.

It is a wise gentlewoman who practises her art with the skill and rigour of a master swordsman. Many a fine gentleman has been led astray by the frantic fluttering of untutored and over-heated young ladies. Take care to be precise in your fanning motions should you wish to avoid ever being misunderstood.

Inspired by an article in *The Spectator*,
Wednesday 27 June 1711

How to Picnic with Elegance and Grace

'YOU MAY FEEL THE URGE TO PLAY A ROUND OF
CROQUET OR SKETCH AN EYE-CATCHING SCENE, OR INDEED
JUST TO BREATHE IN THE FRESHNESS OF THE AIR AND
INDULGE IN THE GAIETY OF YOUR GUESTS.'

Even the most refined and gentle of ladies is apt to feel the constraints of all that social etiquette demands. Though accomplished in her mannerisms and faultless in her execution of the daily rituals of life, a lady, from time to time, may feel an urge to loosen her stays, leave the confines of her parlour and find amusing entertainment in the fresh air of the countryside.

A picnic taken in a serene and picturesque setting, with agreeable friends and a host of splendid delicacies to dine upon can satisfy any lady's craving for casual relaxation and unfettered enjoyment. All careful arrangements and due consideration should be taken to ensure the picnic is a happy and civilised occasion, and one which will attract the most fashionable of guests. It is essential that the locality chosen should offer some interesting feature or outstanding natural scenery. It affords huge pleasure to be able to picnic within the grounds of a stately home, and requests to use such spots are very rarely denied; but permission should first be sought from the owner of the land.

A public spot should be spied out well in advance, in order to ensure its absolute suitability. The site should be accessible, without rocks to stumble upon or steep inclines to ascend. A site that would seem to afford a splendid view from the top of a gentle hill or from the edges of a scenic lake may prove too agitating to ladies of more tender nerves and should be most strenuously avoided. The final place of choosing should be free from anthills or plants of a thorny nature, and should offer much in the way of shade so that the ladies need not employ their parasols for the entirety of the picnic.

Ample provision should be made for the entertainment and comfort of your intrepid guests. A nearby indoor place of resort should be sought out and reserved for use should the weather prove to be unfavourable. An impromptu change of venue will exhilarate your guests and, should the situation arise, your picnic will *not* be deemed an utter failure. Your guests will have received cards of invitation, and you will have provided carriages to convey them to the chosen locality. You must send your servants ahead with a cart of provisions in order that the cloth may be spread and the refreshments arranged for when your guests arrive. Be sure to provide the most popular of dishes such as ribs of beef, fowl, game pie, tongue, crabs and lobster. Cheeses, preserved fruits, pastries, cakes, dinner rolls, strawberries and all manner of refreshing beverages should be plentiful. Be sure to keep your servants at hand to assist upon waiting at the picnic; it affords them a great deal of pleasure, and good and trustworthy servants *must* be rewarded from time to time.

If picnicking in a public place, be sure to engage the services of the local constabulary, as these delightful affairs tend to attract the envious attentions of the lower classes. A police officer on call will discourage the riff-raff from straying too close.

All that remains is for you to relax and enjoy the attentions of every gentleman present, whose solemn duty it is to be amusing and entertaining, and to satisfy a lady's every whim (even if that whim should require him to fetch you a pretty feather from the most inaccessible of places). You are free to sit upon the ground as you choose, but a gentleman is only permitted to follow your example if invited to do so. It is exceedingly pleasant to explore the surrounding countryside, to gather wild flowers and marvel at the butterflies. You may feel the urge to play a round of croquet or sketch an eye-catching scene, or indeed just to breathe in the freshness of the air and indulge in the gaiety of your guests. You must, of course, remain at all times in full sight of the party, so as to avoid any *ruinous* speculation as to your supposed activities.

How to Picnic with Elegance and Grace

It will be most inconvenient for you or any ladies present to lunch whilst holding your parasols, so you must seat yourselves in the shade whilst dining, and take care not to expose your skin to the cruelty of the sun. It is pleasant to end the day with tea at five o'clock and to return home refreshed and invigorated, having made sure to leave final instructions with your servants to clear from the site every sign of frivolity.

Based on Victorian etiquette and household advice manuals

How to Read Tea Leaves

'YOU NEED ONLY TO FLING YOUR CORSET TO ONE SIDE,
DON YOUR MOST ELEGANT TEA GOWN, SEND OUT A FEW
CARDS OF INVITATION AND BE MINDFUL THAT YOUR
REFRESHMENTS ARE NONE TOO ELABORATE.'

The pleasures of afternoon tea shine like a honeyed sun through the genteel society of English ladies. What pastime could, indeed, be more endlessly pleasant than wiling away the hallowed hours in the company of treasured friends and acquaintances? Taking tea is a sociable affair and the very symbol of refinement. It is an opportunity to rest and refresh, and to partake in leisurely and congenial conversation.

It is expected that you should hold at least one 'at home' tea a week; indeed, your social standing depends upon it. Moreover, it is of course a splendid opportunity to display your finest china. You need only to fling your corset to one side, don your most elegant tea gown, send out a few cards of invitation and be mindful that your refreshments are none too elaborate. A vulgar display of garish comestibles is not called for on such an occasion. A selection of teas, thin slices of bread and butter, fancy biscuits, fruits, cakes and other such niceties will suffice.

As hostess it falls to you to entertain your guests, and what could be more satisfying and amusing than to indulge in a few parlour games? By far the most fashionable and fitting is the interpreting of one's fate in the grounds of tea left in the bottom of one's cup. You should first have your butler or waiting man set out all necessary tools for tea-making. The tea caddy (which you will unlock yourself; tea being a most precious commodity), teapot, hot water urn and heater, and of course the teacups, which should be of a light hue and wide-brimmed to allow for greater dispersal of the tea leaves. It is your duty as hostess to brew and serve the tea, and you should take your position at the head of the table. First, pour hot water into the teapot and allow it to sit for a few minutes to warm the pot. Pour this water into a waste bowl and place your favourite blend of tea into the pot and cover with fresh boiling water. Allow to steep for five to eight minutes, then pour unstrained into your guests' teacups and let them sip slowly, instructing them to leave a spoonful of liquid at the bottom of their cups.

Persons who wish to have their futures looked upon should hold their cups by the handle and swirl the remaining contents three times in a clockwise motion, all the while reflecting on a question they desire to be answered. The cup is then turned upside down into the saucer and drained.

You may wish to interpret the tea leaves yourself, or

you may have invited a seasoned reader whose skills can elevate a mundane afternoon to a much talked-about and admired occasion. Whatever the case, the reader will now be handed the drained cup which she will turn back upright and begin to study the various symbols and shapes left behind by the wet clumps of tea leaves.

The reader will hold the cup in her left hand and, starting from the handle (which represents the present time), will start reading the symbols in a clockwise direction to predict events up to a year ahead. Symbols nearest to the rim represent life-changing events, while those near to the bottom are a mere indication of events which may occur. A symbol placed in the very centre of the base of the cup spells great tragedy (you may wish to keep this knowledge to yourself to avoid any of your guests falling into a dead faint).

Common symbols to consider are heart-shaped patterns, which promise love; triangles, which tell of jealousy; star shapes that predict great success and squares indicating a solid character. There are myriad signs that can appear in a drained teacup, from a face, indicating a change in friendship, to a coin, which tells of prosperity, and a cross, which brings reward for suffering.

You need only to practise and trust your instincts and intuition to predict a lady's fortune with the most unerring accuracy, which will leave your guests gasping in awe.

BASED ON *THE HISTORY OF VICTORIAN TEA PARTIES* AND *THE ART OF TASSEOLOGY*

How to Sit for a Portrait

'THE ENGLISH HAVE ESTABLISHED SOMETHING OF A
REPUTATION ABROAD FOR EXCELLING IN THEIR LOVE OF
THEIR OWN IMAGE, AND ONE WOULD DO WELL TO
FOLLOW SUIT IN THIS RESPECT.'

One's place and standing within society cannot today be secured unless one is first immortalised on canvas. The English have established something of a reputation abroad for excelling in their love of their own image, and one would do well to follow suit in this respect. Alas, it cannot be denied that sitting for the artist is most wearisome; all the more so for a lady of good upbringing, for whom securing a representation of herself is to be regarded as the most trivial of vanities. Without tolerating such an undertaking, however, one will simply not be seen to be at one with the latest fashion; neither can one's heir be provided with the most advantageous of public faces. For this purpose, we herein set out our most earnest guidance as to the best method of acquiring said portrait.

Those gentle ladies, for whom pecuniary restrictions are a mere trifle, would be best advised to sojourn in Bath, particularly for the winter season. There, you would do well to seek out the services of one *Thomas Gainsborough*, who is most conveniently situated alongside the Pump Rooms. This location means that you may first take advantage of the waters. (Be advised that the physician will have you sop up such quantities that you must be sure to make *timely* use of the amenities there before the waters make known their presence to you. This is no trivial counsel: we have experience of these facilities as the *least convenient* aspect of the visit, so sparse are they in number and so great is the demand for their occupancy. Nevertheless, it is better that you are called upon to exercise that small degree of patience, and muscular restraint required, in the wait to gain entry to the Pump Room facilities, than to be inconvenienced during your sitting with Mr Gainsborough.)

Mr Gainsborough is a portrait artist of some talent and with a growing respectability amongst the most impressive of aristocratic circles, who has conducted his business out of Bath since 1759. But it is the speed with which he works that is of the greatest attraction to the busy lady. Those for whom he paints have a demanding schedule of social appointments; the Bath season is renowned for its rigours. None can be expected to afford the time for an odiously lengthy sitting. Mr Gainsborough pays respect to this, and furthermore does not allow his swift *modus operandi* to compromise the quality of the finished product. Moreover, his sister (a milliner of some expertise, operating out of the same building) will expertly facilitate a thorough accessorising of one's toilet in readiness for the sitting.

Ensure your attire befits the status you *wish to convey*. Mr Gainsborough can easily make the addition of diamonds and other gems later; the gown, one should strive to get right from the start.

If fate prohibits you from enjoying the benefits of the Bath winter season, and the services of Mr Gainsborough, the miniature has become, of late, a perfectly agreeable form of portraiture that will not preclude the lesser gentlewoman. The fee for such a portrait is considerably more favourable than for a more conventional type, and how gratifying it is to be able to present your friends and acquaintances with your own true likeness in a delightful frame or trinket. A sitting for a miniature with oils can be a delightful affair.

Alternatively, the experience of procuring a miniature shades or shadow portrait is most amusing. It is the most accessible of portraits: a sitting can cost as little as two or three shillings. An ingenious device attached to a chair enables the artist to obtain your profile *in a matter of minutes*, from which he can produce any number of portraits for you to circulate among your friends. A shadow portrait that has been painted on to a chalky plaster will be the most enduring, and for this reason it is currently the method most in mode. (We have heard tell that the artist will mix up pine soot and beer with which to best stain the plaster; we are assured that there is no associated odour such as might be repellent for a lady.) For both types, you will need to pay heed to the manner in which your hair is dressed (or else have the artist select the most flattering and elaborate dressing of your hair that your age and status will allow to be added as embellishments after the sitting), for it will be this alone that will sing of your poise and carriage.

The added beauty of the shadow portrait is that by some wonderment of technology the artist is able to add contemporary fashionable embellishments on to old and out-dated shades. This can be most convenient to a lady for whom appearing to be *à la mode* is essential.

INSPIRED BY AN ARTICLE IN *LADY'S MONTHLY MUSEUM*, OCTOBER 1799

How to Avoid the Parental Consequences of Marital Relations

'A WOMAN MUST FOSTER IN HER HUSBAND AN APPRECIATION
OF THE PRECIOUS NATURE OF HIS GOD-GIVEN EMISSIONS,
RECOGNISING THEM AS BEING BLESSED WITH THE MIRACLE OF
CREATION AND NOT A TRIVIAL SUBSTANCE EXCRETED AT WILL.'

It is only right and fitting that a man and his wife should celebrate their marriage frequently in the privacy of their bedroom. To exercise marital relations goes beyond an expression of love, building a sense of well-being, both in physique and mentality. It refreshes and up-builds the nervous system, prolonging life. However, couples would be well advised to see that they exercise the parental function of marital relations only when they are both of a mind to conceive a child. At all other times, the love function should be exercised with a degree of self-control.

The current perversion of 'preventatives' is both morally abhorrent and unlawful, and is to be avoided at all times and at all costs. Furthermore, their use is far too unrefined for any woman of decorous upbringing to be exposed to, and will coarsen marital relations entirely. Moreover, such unnatural interferences are entirely unreliable, and any child so conceived is liable to be cursed with disagreeable propensities, psychological perversions or physical abnormalities.

A woman must foster in her husband an appreciation of the precious nature of his God-given emissions, recognising them as being blessed with the miracle of creation and not a trivial substance to be excreted at will. Furthermore, she may impress upon him the importance to his health of enjoying marital relations without spilling his creative life-force: for it will be re-circulated around his body and act as a tonic for his nervous system, strengthening his beard and lowering his vocal range.

With time and patience, a devoted husband will learn to separate out the physical from the mental, so that whilst the sense of satisfaction and well-being he derives from marital relations is not diminished, neither is his stock of creative emissions. He must call upon God at the moment of reckoning and entreat Him to supply the strength to enable him to feel at one with pulsating nature whilst not wasting his seed. Failing to call upon the Higher Power at such a moment will, over time, result in *medical harm* to your husband. If a man is to avoid untold damage to his prostate gland and his nervous system, he should first practise the art of establishing contemplative currents of reflective thought along his nerves and across his ganglia. This will thereafter inhibit the throwing off of his seed, much as he might learn to inhibit a blush. A good wife should assist in this rumination, distracting herself and her husband with prayer and hymn at the moment in their relations when it is most pertinent to do so.

Such a divinely appointed ordinance should not be rushed: it will require at least an hour to do it the justice it deserves. In this way, a lady retains her dignity and honour by being free to celebrate her marriage without being exposed to base preventatives and reserves her resolution to practise her parental function until she is so desirous.

BASED UPON THE WRITINGS OF IDA CRADDOCK, LATE
NINETEENTH CENTURY OCCULTIST, HIGH PRIESTESS OF
YOGA AND RELATIONSHIP COUNSELLOR

How to Journey with an Escort

'ANY JOURNEY, HOWEVER WELL PLANNED, CAN SO OFTEN
BE FRAUGHT WITH APPREHENSIONS AND VEXATIONS. IN
LIGHT OF THIS, IT IS ALWAYS MORE DESIRABLE TO
JOURNEY WITH AN ESCORT.'

I t is perfectly acceptable for a lady to journey even considerable distances unaccompanied, so long as the lady conducts herself with propriety. As long as one remembers to pack an abundant supply of grace and humour, to be called upon when one's patience is most tested, one may feel well equipped for the journey.

Any journey, however well planned, can so often be fraught with apprehensions and vexations. In light of this, it is always more desirable to journey with an escort. The well-selected escort will make a lady's journey infinitely more tolerable. For instance, when travelling with an escort, a lady need not trouble herself with any of the practicalities of her trip, such as the baggage, the route or the tickets. One may presume one's escort knows more about travelling than oneself. The escort's duties are plentiful; do your part by ensuring you avoid travelling with a large number of packages. To require your escort to see to more than he can easily carry will risk him inflicting damage to a prized piece, and act as an unwelcome distraction from his other duties. Prior to commencing your journey, it is wise to supply your escort with sufficient money to cover all your anticipated expenses.

An escort should naturally be selected from good stock and have a pleasant and honest demeanour. He should be well known to your family and be of good standing, but the art of selecting an escort lies in the lady's full appreciation of what such a role should entail. An escort will need to first meet you in ample time to obtain your tickets, check your baggage and procure a good seat in the carriage for you. All the while he should look after your hand baggage, assist you in and out of the compartment and make all inquiries about the route.

En route, he should perform many acts of politeness: pointing out objects of interest from the car window and fetching glasses of water or other refreshments, should you be so requisite. If you are averse to conversation, he will need to be sensitive to this and allow you time for private contemplation, or else provide you with stimulating reading matter. The question of reading whilst in motion is one of personal preference: some will advise against in order to preserve the eyesight, whilst many opt to indulge in reading when travelling without any obvious injury. In any case it would be in extremely poor taste for an escort to read if his charge was not doing so.

Upon arrival at your destination, an escort should accompany you to the home of your friends, or to the hotel at which you plan to stop. He should call on you the following day to ascertain how well you are recovered from the journey. Any escort who fails to carry out any of these duties to the satisfaction of his charge should not be called upon to act in such a capacity for any future journey.

Whether travelling alone or under escort, keep money well hidden about your person, leave off any jewellery and desist from constant consultations with your watch. Maintain a level-headed composure at all times. A calm, feminine dignity will usually be sufficient to keep in check the impudence of most young ruffians. Where such advances are not put in their place by your lady-like demeanour, there will always be a well-mannered gentleman to hand that will come to your defence.

ADAPTED FROM ORIGINAL ADVICE IN *YOUTH'S EDUCATOR FOR HOME AND SOCIETY*, BY ANNA R. WHITE, 1896

How to be Delicately Fragrant

'THE VOLUPTUOUS AND HEAVY PERFUME OF MUSK
SHOULD BE AVOIDED AT ALL COSTS. IT IS FAR TOO STRONG
A SCENT, AND LAVISH USAGE CAN CAST DOUBTS UPON
THE WEARER'S STANDARD OF CLEANLINESS.'

The art of maintaining a feminine fragrance requires *fastidiousness* and *discretion*. A lady who does not keep at all times sweet smelling would be reminded that foul odours are harbingers of risk and revulsion, much associated with the unclean, mephitic classes. A perfumed body and an ambrosial home say much about the health and good taste of a true lady. Foul-smelling odours are indicators of illness and you are advised to make liberal use of the many stimulating and refreshing aromas available from Mother Nature's bountiful treasure chest in order to ward off unwelcome diseases.

It is not becoming or indeed attractive to mix scents; a refined woman should reject this temptation and choose only a *single* scent with which to be associated. It is worth remembering that, although popular of late, the voluptuous and heavy perfume of musk should be avoided at all costs. It is far too strong a scent, and lavish usage can cast doubts upon the wearer's standard of cleanliness and, more *alarmingly,* can produce an over-sensitivity in the minds of gentlemen, whose private regions may become distastefully affected. Indeed, any scent derived from animals and associated with base reproductive instincts should be cast aside in favour of more subtle and delicate fragrances.

Many scents derived from Nature have a powerful effect on the constitution and can even enhance the fairness of one's face. The heady scents of lavender, roses, violets and lemon are most popular and delicious.

Once a preferred perfume has been chosen (one suited to your nature and sensibility: for instance, those of tender heart should choose geranium; dark-blue violet for the most pious of ladies; lemon verbena for those of an artistic nature), then you should envelop yourself and all your linen entirely in the same sweet scent. Every aspect of your home and person should be impregnated with a delicious odour, from your laces and handkerchiefs to your bonnet boxes and costumes. Every sheet of notepaper sent out from your desk should tell of your presence before your words have been read. This devotion to detail will surely enhance your attractions.

It is a simple matter to prepare perfumed sachets to place among linen and in closets and cupboards. You merely sprinkle in an abundant manner the perfume of your choice on to small squares of cotton wool. These can then be sewn into muslin bags and trimmed with the prettiest of ribbons and lace. The sachets may be introduced discreetly into the hems of dresses or the folds of sleeves; they can be sewn at collars or in the stays, and even under the cushions of your carriage.

Fresh flowers should be used *prodigiously*, filling the home with a wondrous scent. Many ladies will dry these flowers for use in winter, and then fill their pockets with the scent of summer. Indeed, when passing them by, you would be reminded of a glorious meadow heady with perfume and warm in the glow of a summer's sun! There can be nothing more delightful than stepping into a home filled with the ambience of nature, the very woodwork and drapery steeped in delicious scents.

For your delectation, here follows a recipe for a most harmonious pot-pourri:

> Place a layer of the following aromatic plants and a layer of salt into a pot in an alternating fashion until it is full: rose, orange flowers, lavender, marjoram, thyme, myrtle, melilot, rosemary, laurel, cloves, nutmeg and carnations. Let sit in the sun, stirring the contents every other day. Use after one year.

BASED ON ADVICE GIVEN IN *THE LADY'S DRESSING ROOM,* BY BARONESS STAFFE, TRANS. 1893, LADY COLIN CAMPBELL

How to Use Arsenic Judiciously

'IT IS SAID THAT THE IMBIBING OF AN ARSENIC TONIC
CAN BECOME A HABIT WHICH GROWS UPON A LADY AND
REQUIRES HER TO VISIT THE DRUGGIST FAR MORE
OFTEN THAN IS SEEMLY.'

That arsenic is a wondrous substance we have no doubt. Indeed, its usages in household matters and in the privacy of the boudoir are well known. What fashionable woman of the day does not, on occasion, pay a discreet visit to her local druggist to purchase sixpenneth-worth of powdered arsenic to poison the rats which play havoc with her maidservant's sensibilities? Indeed, what gentlewoman of the home has not had cause to put her neat signature to the druggist's poison book when purchasing a few leaves of fly paper? That the items procured are hardly used for the purposes intended should be no one's business but the buyer's.

It is whispered behind the doors of sweet-smelling boudoirs that judicious use of arsenic can improve the complexion in a woman of beauty beyond belief. We would hesitate to recommend this usage, but have heard it be said that if powdered arsenic is not readily available then soaking fly papers in a quantity of water will cause the arsenic therein to be extracted from the sheet. This liquid can be drunk (in minute doses, of course), or applied directly to the skin to impart a most healthy glow to the complexion and to prevent the creasing of the skin. Some ladies prefer to mix the arsenic with vinegar and chalk, so delirious are they about its skin-whitening properties. It is wise to practise caution in this matter, as it is said that the imbibing of an arsenic tonic can become a habit which grows upon a lady and requires her to visit the druggist far more often than is seemly.

There is a shocking tendency of late for vile hags of the underclasses, those creatures of deviant behaviour with no social standing, to make use of arsenic for the most heinous of crimes. They are driven to poison their children or lovers by passions so fierce they are not of this earth. That these crones should behave in such a manner is abhorrent; but it is you, the gentlewoman of good standing, the guardian angel of her home, who is now suffering the dire consequences of suspicion.

An honest lady is surely at liberty to make use of arsenic for the purposes of beautifying her skin and for ridding her household of vermin? It is undoubtedly the fault of nature if a household is so over-run with rats that *repeated* quantities of arsenic are needed to be brought into the home. No lady of pure heart (even if wed to a husband of tyrannical character) would ever have it in her nature to mix a measure of the powdered poison into her spouse's bedtime cocoa. It would be beyond a true lady's capabilities to select sweet-tasting foods, such as jams and puddings, fruit pies and chocolate, with which to disguise the bitter taste of poison.

A woman of gentle means would *never* let it be known to her acquaintances that her husband has been suffering of late from the most horrendous of gastric pains. If the poor and faithful man should die of his condition, then surely it is God's will? God's will, also, that she be left his inheritance to continue living in the manner he would have wished for her. It is of no interest to a charitable lady, who does nought but sacrifice her every waking moment to secure the happiness of her family within the upper ranks of the godly, to know that good doctors of the day cannot distinguish between a natural death and one laced with poison. It is no fault of the upper classes that women of low rank and dubious character are addicted to the murderous method; a lady of tender mind would *never* consider joining in the practice, however fashionable and profitable it is deemed.

And finally, if your husband should afford you the means by which to refurbish your home with all manner of lavish ornamentations and painted walls of rich hues, we would advise you to avoid the colour known as *Emerald Green*. The arsenic present in its brilliant aspect is said to turn to deadly fumes when a room becomes damp.

Indeed, the chamber of rest becomes a veritable death trap! The *Emerald Green* is a colour most popular within the ornate and sumptuous wallpapers used most often in the bedrooms of gentlemen of taste and fortune. An inconsequential titbit to be sure!

Inspired by the case of Madeleine Smith, tried for the murder, by arsenic poisoning, of her lover (Pierre) Emile L'Angelier, 1857, and the trial of Florence Maybrick, convicted of murder by arsenic poisoning of her husband, James Maybrick, in 1889

How to Cultivate a Physic Garden

'VENUS GOVERNS THE COMPLEXION AND THE ORGANS OF
EVE: HEADY-SCENTED, OSTENTATIOUS AND FLORIFEROUS
PLANTS BEAR HER STAMP ... VENUTIAN PLANTS EXHIBIT
MERCILESSLY PRECOCIOUS FLOWER-HEADS. ITS EFFECTS
ARE WELL-FELT UPON THOSE WISHING TO STIR UP A
MORE PASSIONATE SENSIBILITY.'

No home can run smoothly without it is well supplied by a physic garden that will enable the family to be kept of vigorous well-being.

Whilst your gardener will till the soil and prepare the ground for any fresh planting, it will unquestionably fall upon the lady of the house to ascertain the component parts of the physic garden; the elaborate wit of the apothecary is beyond the command of any gardener. There are some herbs we would deem vital to a well-stocked physic garden:

❋ Lambs Ears is most desirable as its soft, fleecy leaves can be very effectively applied to wounds as a poultice. They have a restorative effect upon the complexion when used in bathing. Have your maidservant harvest a few leaves in the early morning, preferably with the dew still upon them, with which you may bathe your face.

∗ Sage is of curious benefit to the brain, sharpening the senses, strengthening the reflexes and sinews of the body, and cleansing the blood. It will also assist with the treatment of adder bites and, most usefully, dye the hair black, should a lady wish to prolong the looks of her youth. (Furthermore, a decoction of yarrow may be used with which to bathe the scalp so that one may stay the shedding of hair.)

∗ Lovage is an essential plant for any young lady about to enter society. Judiciously used, a distillation of lovage leaves will produce a luminous countenance devoid of spots, freckles and blemishes.

∗ Thyme is a most valuable herb. Applied to a water-bath, it provokes sweats and encourages both urination and vomits, thereby purging the body of any illness. It breaks bladder stones and eases griping stomachs when boiled in wine. In this form, too, it will, moreover, have a positive effect upon madness, sluggish stupors and any agitation of the passions. A decoction of thyme will also help rid a person of worms and warts.

Further to this small guidance, we urge that a lady be governed in the intricate design of any physic garden by the work of Dr Nicolas Culpeper, whose *Complete Herbal* is indispensable. Culpeper insists it is more than the physical resemblances of the herb that signify its use, as has been hitherto put forth. The *astrology of the skies* governs the medicinal properties of every plant. Moreover, all parts of the body are, in turn, influenced by an astrological body. Marry the two, says Culpeper, and you will secure a most speedy treatment of any disease, even without the intervention of any physician or apothecary.

* *Venus* governs the complexion and the Organs of Eve: heady-scented, ostentatious and floriferous plants bear her stamp. Venus is always prompt in the display of her beauty: likewise Venutian plants exhibit mercilessly precocious flowerheads. Its effects are well-felt upon those wishing to stir up a more passionate sensibility.

* *Mars* governs all things stimulant, sour and sustaining for the muscles and the thrust of the body. For vitality and healthy blood, it is essential that every physic garden contains the herbs pertaining to Mars.

* Those plants that have the hue or form of the *Sun*, such as calendula, will be most efficacious in the treatment of the heart and the circulation. Here, too, are those plants that track the course of the sun with their heads,

such as the heliotrope. Plants that give off heat, such as the clove, will also act as an energiser for the heart.

* The *Moon* steeps the fluids of the earth in its liquid potency; likewise those many plants bearing fruits that are luscious and rotund exhibit the lunar hallmark. In turn, it follows that lunar influences are most strong upon the secretions and fluids of the body; any herb that acts upon the body by drawing sweats and per-spirations are similarly acting on the moon's behalf. It is by the saturation and succulence of the plant that you will most readily identify the influence of the moon.

* *Jupiter* has a bearing upon the system of digestion and therefore under its influence grow all things edible. Those herbs, plants, nuts and seeds that fall under the sway of Jupiter will act upon all digestive spasms and ease griping and warbling bellies.

* *Mercury*'s sign is readily detected in the forked or divided leaf, and the distinctively tart aroma, such as with fennel or dill. These will have a most pleasing effect upon the nerves. A nosegay of such herbs and flowers will elevate the spirits following a fright or other intelligence of a disturbing nature, whereupon a person could thereafter become oppressed with melancholy. (In which instance, the application of

garlic chives must be avoided *at all costs*, on the advice of Dr Culpeper.)

✳ *Saturn* influences the process by which we grow heavy with the signs of age. When Saturn acts upon a plant, it creates a poison. Thus the deadly belladonna and hemlock are Saturn's harvest. Used with caution, however, the plants of Saturn can relieve pain and induce a restorative sleep.

Clearly, a lady must study well the planning of her medicinal herb garden. Consider the uses you and your family will most commonly have need of, and accommodate those within your design. Be governed in all things by the wit of one greater than you in these matters: Dr Culpeper.

INSPIRED BY THE POPULARITY OF THE
SEVENTEENTH CENTURY HERBAL HANDBOOK,
CULPEPER'S *COMPLETE HERBAL*

How to Cope with Your Confinement

'CHILDBIRTH IS A DANGEROUS OCCUPATION ... YOU MAY WISH
TO BID A TENDER FAREWELL TO YOUR DEAREST FAMILY AND
FRIENDS, LEST YOU SHOULD NOT SURVIVE THE LABOUR.'

Childbirth is an obligation incumbent upon all healthful women. It is a God-given process and is, indeed, the sole object for which the fairer sex was created. Society is correct in believing that producing a son and heir is a service a good and dutiful wife owes to her husband. Childbearing is without question a gentlewoman's *only* correct occupation.

The perils of childbirth are numerous, and once it becomes discernible that you are feeling more than a *little delicate*, you must withdraw yourself from public inspection and be confined to the privacy of your bedroom and parlour. A little feminine deceit will allow you to prolong your freedom in society if you continue to keep a fashionable toilet and pull your stays in tight over your protruding abdomen. However, as soon as your true condition has been noted by those around you, then you have little choice but to don an invalid gown and remain out of sight.

As a lady of good standing, you will find it is necessary, during the final weeks of your confinement, to leave the quietude of the country and travel to town to stay with your most eminent of friends. These dear people will be called upon to prepare their house to accommodate you (as the expectant mother), your husband, friends, family, the physician and all his assistants. You will, of course, have made sure to engage the services of a discreet and, above all, competent physician with no deaths upon his conscience. Childbirth is a dangerous occupation: you would do well to surround yourself with only the best assistance money can procure. You may wish to bid a tender farewell to your dearest family and friends, lest you should not survive the labour.

By giving birth in town you can be certain that the news will be made public almost immediately and your name will once more be upon the lips of every person of importance.

It is prudent to bring with you your own delivery bed. You may have one that has been in the family for generations and passed down to you from your own mother and grandmother. Even if birthing at home, it is as well to deliver a baby on a separate bed than the one it was conceived upon. It is lewd and unseemly to be reminded of marital relations when involved in the *spiritual* act of childbirth. You must preserve your modesty at all times during labour. A cotton shift worn tucked up under the arms and a short petticoat placed about the hips are sufficient to ensure your continued purity. The petticoat can be removed once soiled after the birth and the cotton shift immediately pulled down. You must lie on the left side of your body with your knees pulled up to your abdomen and with your back to the physician. This will save both of you the discomfiture of seeing the other's face.

Be under no illusion: the pains of childbirth are immense but a skilful physician will draw your blood to ease the distress and quieten you down. It has been noted that some physicians are turning to the use of ether and chloroform to deaden the pains of labour. This is an abhorrent practice and much against the will of God; indeed, suffering through childbirth is *essential* to bring about and further develop a deep maternal love.

How to Cope with Your Confinement

You should lie in bed for up to six weeks after delivery and use the time wisely in learning how to be affectionate, caring and nurturing towards your child, as is now the fashion to be. You will be attended to during this period by a monthly nurse whose strength and bodily vigour will enable her to perform all *necessary duties* in order to keep yourself and the newborn child in a comfortable and happy condition. Once your strength is regained, you may attend church to be religiously cleansed and to thank God for your survival; only then will you be ready to be accepted once more into the waiting arms of society.

ADAPTED FROM *THE HISTORY OF VICTORIAN WOMEN'S HEALTH ISSUES: CHILDBEARING IN THE BRITISH ARISTOCRACY, 1760–1860* BY JUDITH S. LEWIS

How to Secure a Proposal of Marriage

'WHILST IT IS TRUE THAT IN MARRIAGE LIES NOT A
WOMAN'S ONLY CHANCE OF HAPPINESS, NEVERTHELESS
THEREIN IS FOUND HER VERY BEST.'

You may be certain there is nothing so false as to assume that one's only path to happiness in life lies in securing a good marriage. There are many hundreds of women who find moments of some comfort in the interminable solitude and relentless seclusion of spinsterhood. Moreover, to exhibit a coarse and unseemly impatience to be wed is to adopt the surest way to spinsterhood. There is nothing a gentleman may find more repellent in a young lady than her thinly veiled hunger for a well-titled husband (more so, should such an ambition be detected in a lady of years advancing well beyond the inaugural year of her third decade).

That is not to say, however, that we do not advocate, *in*

the strongest terms, that you seek to secure a proposal of marriage from the very highest calibre of gentleman available to you, and at the earliest possible opportunity. Whilst it is true that in marriage lies not a woman's *only* chance of happiness, nevertheless therein is found her very *best*. A wise union will open up a life of comfort, respectability and rank beyond anything that may be anticipated without him.

Be sure that you consider our counsel before you are tempted to accept the first offer you are presented with simply to satiate your desire to snag a husband. Heaven forbid your enthusiasm should ever cause you to relinquish the relative ease and independence of a single life for the sake of a life of servitude to a barrel-bellied autocrat or, worse, a witless blockhead.

Be sure in your search to reject any who will entail upon your future offspring a madness, or any other hereditary disease. Avoid, too, the rake and the fool. Both will be the cause of much public embarrassment; the former will have but a low opinion of his wife, resultant from frequent encounters with the most unsavoury of our sex. The latter will be so jealous of his wife's wit that he will behave in the most absurd of manners.

You would do well to cast all thoughts of romantic love out of your head: without more than your fair share of good fortune, it is unlikely you will marry for love. Love is that which your *suitor* will declare he is consumed with whenever he is in mind of you. Any man of wit and taste will offer marriage to the lady he loves above all other. This preference he expresses for you will flatter, all the more so if he is a gentleman upon whom you have already bestowed a share of your esteem. You may be sure that there will be scant few of these gentlemen: how much less probable is it that among these few is to be found the one your heart most approves of?

Thus, when you find yourself flattered by the attentions of one with whom you share some compatibility of taste, you may accept his proposal secure in the knowledge that from this position, friendship and affection may blossom. Any lady of refinement and grace will marry because she *admires* her suitor and, naturally, because she is grateful that he has expressed his preference for her above all others.

When you perceive in a gentleman an *excess* of good manners and an inability to appear anything other than *solemn* in your company, where previously you have known him to be of good humour, you may rest assured his heart is filled with love and admiration for you. If he is of a disposition that is agreeable to you, call upon all your reserves of patience; he is certain to make known his intentions in due course.

On no account should you reveal to him the full mark of your affections; less still if you reciprocate his love! No good will ever come of fierce or passionate love; do not surrender to it! Such a union cannot endure long before it becomes a thing of mutual abhorrence and revulsion.

ADAPTED FROM *A FATHER'S LEGACY TO HIS DAUGHTERS* BY
DR GREGORY OF EDINBURGH, 1774

How to Hire a Governess

'A GOVERNESS IS, BY HER VERY NATURE, A SPINSTER.
SEE THAT SHE REMAINS THAT WAY.'

To those ladies of noble households, mindful of the education of their children, we urge that you pay the most careful attention to the hiring of a governess. There can be no other duty incumbent upon a mother of greater significance than that of making certain one's offspring are properly diverted by a governess of reputable breeding.

A good marriage to a man of exalted station is not without its crosses. A wife is obliged to linger over the perfecting of her morning toilet, and to change her attire as often as four times daily. The hours after luncheon are necessarily taken up with the promenade and other preoccupations suited to a lady (by which we respectfully suggest needlepoint, watercolours, piano playing and the learning of French, with which one may endlessly amuse one's parlour guests). Furthermore, she has the odious task of seeing that her household is constantly and adequately staffed, thereby removing all danger of any vulgar chores falling into her direct remit. In short, the time of a true lady is to be seen to be taken up with *nothing of import*! Anything that may be interpreted as labour or toil, along with anything that suggests an intellectual bent not naturally attributed to ladies of good birth, would be improprietous in the extreme.

Nothing can be more tiresome, in that it impinges upon these decorous pursuits, than the issue of educating one's offspring. It cannot be permitted to occupy one's thoughts or daylight hours beyond that it necessitates the hiring of the governess. With this in mind, we herein set out some points of guidance that you may be all the more facilitated in a speedy resolution:

1. Always select a lady from a gentle, if not a noble, family. She will take on the full responsibility of preparing your sons and daughters to take up their rightful place in society and cannot be expected to be equipped for this task if she has not originated in that society.

2. She will very likely be orphaned, or at least without a father; hence her current disappointed circumstances. Most desirable are the orphaned young daughters of clergymen; failing that, one can usually find success in searching out an officer's widow, for

they are always in plentiful supply. Both types will have an excellent education and finely honed sense of decorum in their favour sufficient to school your children. Be not discouraged by her pecuniary loss: her misfortune is, after all, the source of your fortunate gain.

3. Her breeding will demand that she is allocated her own maid. Ensure that her quarters are adequate for a lady of her birth: she must not be permitted to forget her breeding, lest she lack in her ability to pass on to your children those elements of social grace for which she has been hired. She may dine alone in her quarters, or with the children. Rarely, and by way of reward, she will be gratified by the opportunity to dine with you and the master. She will not be welcome with the servants as she is not of their class.

4. A governess is, by her very nature, a spinster. See that she remains that way. Do not tolerate any relations with suitors.

5. Above all else, look to the facial characteristics of your governess. She should be plain, though not disfigured. Preferably of brunette hair: on no account hire a red-headed governess, least of all one with naturally coiled red hair! Both are indications of an iniquitous and

licentious character. In this respect, you would do well to ensure your governess is neither fair of face, nor of hair: by such an error have many husbands and sons been led astray!

INSPIRED BY THE PORTRAYAL OF THE GOVERNESS IN
EIGHTEENTH- AND NINETEENTH CENTURY FICTION

How to Cure Common Ailments

'THE COMMON SYMPTOMS OF WORMS ARE AN ITCHING
OF THE NOSE AND SEAT, A HARD, SWOLLEN BELLY, A
VORACIOUS APPETITE, A PALENESS OF COUNTENANCE
AND A STINKING BREATH.'

It befalls all ladies of a certain breeding to be called upon at various times in their lives to perform the duties of a sick nurse. It is most advantageous to be prepared for these occasions by familiarising oneself with the nature of, and remedies for, the most commonplace of maladies. As a woman, your kind temperament, docile manners, neat-handedness and mercy towards the suffering render you the model sick-bed companion. Your desire to relieve misery and your blindness to the disgusts of a sick room lend all credence to the worthiness of the fairer sex.

Ignorance and excessive living can be held responsible for all manner of ills, but there are many precautions which can be taken to avoid the loss of health. Nothing is more conducive to a sound constitution than abstinence, plain food and a due degree of exercise. There are many of tender nerves and nature who, although constant in their precautions, are none the less subjected to a frequency of disorders. It is to these unfortunates that you must administer your attentions.

In the first stage of sickness there may be some doubt and perplexity as to the exact nature of the malady (if there seems to be a complication of disorders then a God-fearing physician must be sent for), but certain arrangements can be made whilst waiting for the sickness to develop. The patient must be put immediately to bed in a thoroughly ventilated room; the air as fresh and as sweet as that outside, but kept warm by a well-supplied fire. The sufferer must be attended to at all times and should be offered the blandest of foods and the coolest of wines at regular intervals.

A fever that begins with chilliness, heat, thirst and restlessness then succeeds to a violent pain in one side is very likely to be a pleurisy. It is a fact known to every person of some intelligence that when a fever is accompanied by a hard and fast pulse, then bleeding will be necessary. Pleurisy requires a large amount of blood to be drawn at the very onset of symptoms; at least 12 to 14 ounces. Warm, young cabbage leaves applied to the sides of the patient will draw off a little moisture and may decrease the pain. A diet that encourages purging but offers little nourishment is to be recommended. A decoction of figs, raisins and barley water would be most proper.

A whooping cough can prove fatal to children, but seldom seems to affect adults. Its symptoms are so well known they need hardly be described. There are many effectual remedies; the most greatly recommended being that of woodlice and millipedes. The insects should be bruised then left to infuse overnight in a pint of white wine. The resulting liquor should then be strained and a tablespoonful given to the patient three or four times daily. Garlic ointment, mixed with an equal quantity of hog's lard, should be spread upon rags and applied to the feet; this is an exceedingly good remedy for the most obstinate of patients.

When a stuffing of the nose, a pain in the head and a heavy weariness is complained of, it is likely that the perspiration has been obstructed and the patient is with cold. He should be made to lie longer in bed and fed only water-gruels sweetened with honey, chicken broth, or barley and liquorice decoctions. This practice quite often carries off a cold in a day or two, but if treatment is neglected or delayed then the disease can gather strength and emerge as a fatal consumption of the lungs. There are those who will attempt to cure a cold by consuming vast quantities of strong liquor. This practice is not to be recommended, as although in some cases a drunken stupor can restore the flow of perspiration, in others the malady may be increased and the common cold turned into an inflammatory fever.

The common symptoms of worms are an itching of the nose and seat, a hard, swollen belly, a voracious appetite, a paleness of countenance and a stinking breath. There may also be palpitations of the heart, swooning and other nervous disorders. No disease so frequently confounds the physician's skill, yet all agree that strong purgatives are necessary for the expulsion of the vermin. Sea water is an excellent remedy but when it cannot be obtained then common salt dissolved in water should be drunk. Oily medicines are very beneficial in the expelling of worms, and salad oil and salt, mixed with a glass of red port may be taken thrice a day or as often as the stomach will bear it. White soap mixed in pottage, garlic, tansy and rue are also all good against the worms. But patients should be advised that the surest way to preserve themselves from worms is to take plenty of fresh air and to avoid eating raw herbs and roots.

By far the greatest medicine is the love of God, as this

keeps all passions within due bounds and it is only when the passions become disordered that miseries and sicknesses prevail.

ADAPTED FROM *DOMESTIC MEDICINE OR THE FAMILY PHYSICIAN*, 1785, BY DR WILLIAM BUCHAN (1729–1805)

How to Promenade

'"THE CUT" IS PERMISSIBLE ONLY WHERE YOU WISH TO
EXCUSE YOURSELF FROM THE PERSISTENT BOWING OF A
GENTLEMAN WHOSE ACQUAINTANCE ... YOU DO NOT WISH TO
KEEP UP. A SILENT, ICY GLARE SHOULD SUFFICE TO
PORTRAY YOUR DISTASTE.'

The Promenade is an agreeable practice for a lady, providing, as it does, an opportunity for taking the air and exercising the limbs with grace, as well as exhibiting one's grasp of all things decorous. Hence, for all who wish to be perceived in the very highest social esteem, we have here assembled sound guidance of all that is to be adhered to and avoided whilst promenading.

Be sure your attire is that which most befits a morning toilet. A simple silk, or similar lightweight fabric of dark hue, with spotless cuffs and collar, is most appropriate. Reserve your plunging necklines and transparent fabrics for evening engagements. Similarly, see that your adornments are appropriate: one should never be seen in diamonds or pearls before dinner. A watch and a well-chosen brooch should suffice.

Naturally, you should never appear in the street without your gloves, which should fit with a flawless perfection. Such details will ensure that your dress does not attract undue attention, much less elicit unpleasant remarks.

Whilst promenading, be sure that your skirts do not drag along the walkway, as this is a source of much annoyance to other pedestrians. And at all costs, refrain from eyeing the dress of another so intently as to appear to inspect its very stitching. It is preferable that any unmarried lady below the age of 30 refrain from walking alone wherever practicable. Possible exceptions are the walk to church, or an early-morning promenade around the park. Even here, however, it is wise to walk in the company of another lady, man or servant.

If you are accompanied, be sure to avoid walking more than two abreast as this will absorb too much of the walkway and present an inconvenience to others. Always pass oncoming pedestrians by the right. If you are in the company of a gentleman, he will usually give you the inner path, so as to avoid you being jostled by passers-by. Should such a jostling occur, and where the offender makes his apologies to you, you may thereafter acknowledge him with nothing more than a cold bow.

Your gentleman escort should see to it that he adapts his pace so as to accommodate yours. Pay heed that he walk without any ungainly swing of the arm or stride.

Such a characteristic is not genteel. There may arise an occasion of some urgency where you find yourself faced with the temptation to walk at speed. *Do not succumb:* it is most difficult to combine speed with grace, and the latter should never be sacrificed. You may accept the arm of a gentleman only after dark, or in other circumstances where safety dictates it is wise to do so. A gentleman may take the arm of two ladies; the reverse is never acceptable.

There are strict conditions governing a lady's decision to exercise her exclusive right to 'The Cut' (that is, to refuse to acknowledge an acquaintance). An unmarried lady should never cut one who is already married, nor should any lady cut a near relation or member of the clergy. When promenading, see that you are prompt to acknowledge all friends and acquaintances with a delicate smile and a slight bow of the head.

A gentleman who has not first been formally introduced, should never risk initiating a salutation upon meeting you. Such a breach of etiquette would expose him to much embarrassment. 'The Cut' is permissible only where you wish to excuse yourself from the persistent bowing of a gentleman whose acquaintance you have not made, or else do not wish to keep up. A silent, icy glare should suffice to portray your distaste. Reserve as the very last resort, the most extreme response: 'Sir, I have not the honour of your acquaintance.'

How to Promenade

❧

Adapted from original advice given in *Ladies' and Gentlemen's Etiquette: A Complete Manual of the Manners and Dress of American Society* by Mrs E. B. Duffey, 1877, and other Victorian etiquette manuals

How to Enhance the Profile of Your Nose

'A NOSE-SHAPER WORKS PARTICULARLY WELL ON FLAT,
UP-TURNED AND ONE-SIDED NOSES, OR ON DISTENDED
AND OBJECTIONABLE NOSTRILS.'

A pleasing profile is essential to any lady of good standing, whatever her age, and the importance in *appearance* of a lady's nose in relation to the beauty and symmetry of her face can never be overestimated. Even a slight deformity of this prominent feature can disfigure the whole countenance and impair any prospects of a good marriage.

For ladies unfortunate enough to be encumbered by a nose of unsightly prominence or deformity, there is a device specifically designed to re-fashion the offending feature back into a more pleasing and acceptable form. The device works particularly well on flat, up-turned and one-sided noses, or on distended and objectionable nostrils.

Fortunately, such deformities can be remedied by applying a gentle but continuous pressure and the 'nose-shaper' has the means to bring about remarkable results in a way that is mercifully painless to the user.

The 'nose-shaper' is comprised of a main body portion of thin, yielding metal made comfortable to the wearer by the addition of a soft chamois covering. The shaper is worn over the nose and is yielding enough to be bent into a shape of desirable proportions. An additional projecting tongue can be bent into position under the tip of the nose pressing upon the cartilage and assisting in the delicate re-shaping of the nostrils.

The whole device is held in place by bands secured to the shaper. These can be positioned where most beneficial and should be pulled firmly around to the back of the head, where they can be crossed over then passed to the front of the head to be fastened about the forehead with a buckle. The secured bands should firmly grip the nose on both sides resulting in a gentle but steady pressure on the now-condensed protuberance. This pressure will, over time, allow the nose to be re-shaped into a more charming form.

When dealing with a one-sided nose (that is to say, one which prefers to stray to the left or right rather than keeping to a central alignment), one side of the main body portion of the shaper can be bent to a greater or lesser degree in order to remedy the particular fault. The beauty of this device is that it will lend itself to the correction of *almost any* olfactory disfigurement.

How to Enhance the Profile of Your Nose

Many ladies find it preferable to wear the shaper at night whilst in the confines of their chamber, but it is comfortable enough to be worn during the day in the private realm of the parlour when not entertaining, and will not prevent engagement in any light domestic activity. It can be removed at a moment's notice if callers arrive unexpectedly, but continuous use is advised to ensure the desired result in a comparatively short period of time.

BASED ON A DEVICE PATENTED BY IGNATIUS NATHANIEL SOARES, 23 APRIL 1907

How to Prepare and Cook a Calf's Head

'TOWARDS THE END OF THE JAW BONE LAYS THE SWEET-
BREAD OF THE THROAT, WHICH IS A DELICATE MORSEL AND
QUITE THE MOST ESTEEMED PART OF THE HEAD.'

A well-dressed calf's head is a most popular entrée to serve discerning guests. It should not be presented as the main dish but should follow the soup and precede the roast. A genteel, if small, dish, a calf's head is best appreciated when the head is young, fat and cleanly white.

Firstly, remove the tongue and brains, and soak the head in changes of cold water for a good few hours. Then simmer gently in a savoury bouillon until tender and flavoursome. Once cooked, the head should first be cut into along the fleshy part of the cheekbone. A good quantity of *handsome* slices may be found here. Towards the end of the jaw bone lays the sweetbread of the throat, which is a delicate morsel and quite the most esteemed part of the head.

How to Prepare and Cook a Calf's Head

Many persons have a keen taste for the eye; this can be cut from its orbit by driving the point of a carving knife deep into the edge of the socket and cutting right around so as to release the meat from the bone. The eye may be divided so as to oblige more than one person. On the underside of the roof of the calf's mouth is a thick, white, crinkled skin. This is the palette, which can be readily peeled off the bone and set aside to be enjoyed cold at some later date. There is plenty of good meat to be found on the underside of the jaw and a quantity of flavoursome gristle to be pared off the ears. This method of preparation is the simplest way to enjoy the delicate parts of a calf's head, but to truly titillate the eye and palate of your guests a calf's head can be served *en tortue*, that is to say, garnished with a tantalising arrangement of all manner of sweetbreads, cockscombs, cocks, kidneys, truffles, crayfish and eggs.

After removing the meat from the cooked head dice it into cubes and simmer over a low heat with a quantity of *Sauce à la Tortue*. Boil lightly the brains and tongue until tender. A browned croustade of rice should be placed on a platter and surrounded by the diced calf's head meat. The tongue and brains can be sliced neatly and placed in a pleasing manner atop the croustade. The *Sauce à la Tortue* is poured over this arrangement, then the whole dish garnished in as extravagant a manner as possible with alternating designs using the afore-mentioned sweetbreads, cockscombs, truffles, crayfish, eggs, cocks, kidneys and gherkins.

How to Prepare and Cook a Calf's Head

The simple receipt for Sauce à la Tortue

Pour into a shallow pan one glassful of dry Madeira. Add to this some finely chopped ham, a pinch of mignonette, pimento, cayenne and a chopped shallot. Simmer gently, then add two spoons of consommé and a little tomato sauce. Bring to the boil, strain through a cloth and just before serving add a little butter.

There are plentiful versions of this dish, but be assured it has satisfied many a royal diner and is sure to become a celebrated addition to your culinary repertoire.

ADAPTED FROM A NINETEENTH CENTURY RECIPE SERVED TO QUEEN VICTORIA BY ROYAL CHEF CHARLES ELME FRANCATELLI (1805-1876)

How to Fashion and Decipher a Tussie-Mussie

'AS NO LADY WOULD WISH HER CAREFULLY PREPARED
TOILETTE TO BE SPOILED BY THE STAINS OF WET MOSS, IT
IS AS WELL SHE ACQUIRES A SUITABLE POSY HOLDER IN
WHICH TO HOUSE HER TUSSIE-MUSSIE.'

How the heart of every lady blesses the flower! How abundantly the rapturous blossoms have encircled the cradle, altar and tomb with their divine fragrance and otherworldly beauty! It is only fitting, then, that these delights of nature should have a language of their very own; how enchanting and fortuitous it is that we may harness this language to our own advantage. As every woman of passionate nature is aware, it is against the rules of propriety to voice your most heartfelt sentiments towards an admired acquaintance. How wonderful therefore that there is a method whereby a gentleman can speak freely to a lady, conveying his deepest affections whilst remaining eloquently silent! Indeed, how much more delightful that a lady may respond to these approaches in a manner which will never compromise her standing in society!

A small selection of flowers, fashioned into the prettiest of tussie-mussies, can tell a lover's tale in scented words. A judiciously chosen flower can woo, melt or indeed break a heart. A lady of culture should study well the language of flowers and learn how to affect an admirable tussie-mussie; the genteel and popular conveyor of sentiment and affection. But the giving or receiving of a tussie-mussie is not limited to would-be lovers alone. Indeed, it is entirely appropriate for friends and family to exchange these most captivating nosegays. You may send out your greetings, compliments, even your reprimands, without ever having to lay eyes upon the receiver.

No respectable lady should leave home or attend a fashionable social gathering without the finest of tussie-mussies fastened to her person, and as no lady would wish her carefully prepared toilet to be spoiled by the stains of wet moss, it is as well she acquires a suitable posy holder in which to house her tussie-mussie. It is every woman's ambition to own several of these tiny holders to be worn either tucked in the *décolletage*, at the waist or in the hair. One's family jeweller may be commissioned to fashion the most coveted inset with turquoise or made in gilt, vermeil or sterling. It warms a lady's heart when her posy holder attracts the envious glances of her dear friends.

The fashioning of a tussie-mussie is a delightful task; indeed, how can any person not derive pleasure from working hand-in-hand with nature's bounty? You must first gather together the individual flowers and herbs that you wish to include in your posy. Many appropriate blooms may be found in the garden or along country roads. An unusual bloom, or one which is not to be found in the vicinity of your estate but is none the less vital to the conveying of your message, may be ordered discreetly from your florist. A central flower is needed, along with filler flowers and herbs such as rosemary, lavender, violets, baby's breath, ivy and mint. Larger leaves, such as lamb's ears or sweet-scented geranium leaves, may be used to frame the outside of your tussie-mussie. The whole arrangement, when complete, should be wrapped in damp moss and a doily, then secured with small pins or tied with a lovers' knot.

The meanings associated with certain plants and flowers are rooted in the deep sods of time. Dear Shakespeare himself had a hand in the art! Those meanings familiar to most are rose (denoting love), lily (purity), ivy (friendship and fidelity), rosemary (remembrance) and sweet violet (modesty). Many meanings will be less familiar, such as briars (denoting envy), acacia (concealed love), buttercup (riches) and cypress and marigold (despair). There are many floriography dictionaries available for you to educate yourself in the rich language of the botanist.

Consider the conversation that follows and make haste to compose your own unique tussie-mussie:

Moss Rosebud, Meadow Lychnis and Amethyst: 'I admire your education and think I have fallen in love with you.'

Spiderwort, Marjoram, Betony and Southernwood: 'You must pardon my behaviour; I was under the influence of wine and am afraid I have misled you. Your feelings are not returned.'

Vine, Great Bindweed, Almond and Mimosa: 'I am deeply wounded and abhor your drunken behaviour.'

Bee Ophrys, Humble Plant, Clotbur, Henbane and Hazel: 'I am an utter oaf and beg your forgiveness.'

Swallow-wort, Fir, Cloves and Yellow Tulip: 'My love for you lingers but time will heal my sorrow.'

Acalia May, Flos Adonis and Volkamenia: 'I have mended

my ways and will never behave in such a manner again. I wish much happiness upon you.'

Convolvus Major, Hyacinth and Arbor Vitae: 'I no longer harbour any hopes for your love but am content to be your friend.'

INSPIRED BY *COLLIER'S CYCLOPEDIA OF COMMERCIAL AND SOCIAL INFORMATION AND TREASURY OF USEFUL AND ENTERTAINING KNOWLEDGE*, COMPILED BY NUGENT ROBINSON AND P. F. COLLIER, 1882. ALSO *LE LANGAGE DES FLEURS* BY CHARLOTTE DE LA TOUR, 1818

How to Respond to a Proposal of Marriage

'A LADY NEITHER EXPLAINS NOR COMPLAINS; IN A REFUSAL
OF MARRIAGE AS, INDEED, IN LIFE. HOWEVER ... THERE ARE
THOSE GENTLEMEN WHOSE CONDUCT CALLS FOR A DEGREE
OF CONTROLLED, CONSIDERED, BUT NONE THE LESS
ENTIRELY VOICED OUTRAGE.'

⋘⋙

An honourable and genuine passion in a true gentleman is a thing too challenging to counterfeit. A lady will be governed best by her wit and instinct in responding to any who make known their advances. Your prerogative as a lady of good stock is to accept or decline. If your inclination is to accept his hand, then let decorum govern the contents of your letter of acceptance (for you would be wise to make your reply in writing and only after a pause of some appropriate time).

Refusal will be a matter of much more delicacy. Here follows guidance in the form of standards of letter that you may call upon as required:

Refusal on the basis of antipathy or abhorrence

This will be of particular use in the case of a gentleman whose behaviour – in business, for example – is worthy of some reproof.

Sir –

Your address has been the cause of much astonishment on my part. That one who has behaved so detrimentally to his reputation can have the effrontery to attempt to demolish my good name in marriage is beyond comprehension. Had you taken a moment to mull over your proposal, you may have easily observed that your agency in this affair has earned you, not my love or affection, but rather my permanent and unalterable dislike.

Refusal on the basis that the reputation of the suitor is in jeopardy

Too many of our young men today are finding the temptations of town bachelorhood overpowering. Business matters have taken them into the city and away from the protective influence of their mothers. This can only result in an unsteadiness of character which renders them entirely unsuitable as a husband. Be firm in your response, that they may waste no other young lady's time but rather divert their efforts towards widows or else to spinsters more advanced in years, whose limited options may make them more apt to overlook such traits.

Sir –

Your behaviour has affected the cerebral and physical disquiet of too many young ladies over recent times to enable me to respond to your address in any way that is sympathetic or positive. You are, in my opinion, perilous to young ladies of good upbringing, and as such I may neither accept your proposal nor any longer consider you an intimate acquaintance. No man with such wanton disregard for the respect due to the weaker sex can be in a position to offer happiness.

Refusal on the basis that the suitor is too young in respect to one's own age

Should you be in the lamentable position of being a widow approached by such unsavoury characters as have been alluded to above, you may be grateful of the opportunity to draw upon the following letter.

Sir –

I am, as I am sure you are aware, a lady of mature years. I have in my custody both children and a sizeable estate, the nurture and protection of which I am solely responsible. In this respect, I am able to make two objections to your address that I am quite confident you will not be able to surmount. Firstly, your youth and reputation not only go against you but also prohibit you from providing any paternal guidance for my children. Furthermore, the estate is mine merely to safeguard for my heir; had I accepted your proposal, you could put any thought of benefiting from it far from your mind. I am quite sure that therein lay your only motive for proposing marriage to one such as I. Consider your conscience, sir! May you feel the shame your behaviour surely warrants!

There is much to be said for exercising that feminine restraint for which our sex has become renowned. In truth, a lady neither explains nor complains; in a refusal of marriage as, indeed, in life. However, it is only right that we should make it known that there are those (mercifully few) gentlemen whose conduct sometimes calls for a degree of controlled, considered, but none the less *entirely voiced* outrage of the sort that only a woman's well-crafted letter can duly deliver.

ADAPTED FROM ORIGINAL ADVICE IN *THE WORCESTER LETTER WRITER*, 1879, DICK & FITZGERALD, NEW YORK

How to Enjoy the Indian Weed with Propriety

'THE ART OF ENJOYING THE SNUFF LIES IN THE DELICACY WITH WHICH THE THUMB AND FOREFINGER CAN BE EMPLOYED TO SECURE A PINCH OF THE POWDER.'

Any lady of propriety must avoid and abhor the *smoking* of the Indian Weed as a low and ill-fitting act. Let such a sight be restricted to women of artisanal or Celtic origin. A lady must be influenced in this matter by the politesse of the Royal Court. Since the reign of Queen Elizabeth, the delicate inhalation of a pinch of perfumed snuff has been the mode. (Indeed, Queen Charlotte was a devotee of some reputation, known by all at Court as 'Snuffy Charlotte'.)

The art of enjoying the snuff lies in the delicacy with which the thumb and forefinger can be employed to secure a pinch of the powder. A lady should do so gracefully and deftly, holding the pinch to her nostril and inhaling without drawing attention to herself. This may then be followed with a discreet sneeze. To be wholly assured that you have perfected the art with femininity, rehearsal in front of the glass is essential prior to public presentation.

On no account request to share the snuff of another, although if offered it is perfectly acceptable to partake. Wiser still, be sure to carry enough about your person. Keep a larger box in the drawing-room with which you can keep yourself, and your guests, well stocked.

The box in which you choose to carry the snuff is of the utmost importance. Avoid coarse boxes crafted out of horn, and beware the current fashion in some circles for boxes which open to reveal portraits of women in the most flagrant of poses. Choose the most tasteful box your pecuniary circumstances will allow. An artfully crafted floral *Limoges* box, or a perfectly engraved golden one will sing of your taste and social standing more than any gown or jewel may do.

In some aristocratic circles, the preference is to carry a different snuffbox for every day of the year, altering to suit the season, the weather or the occasion. While this may be a little extravagant for a lady of less than regal status, it illustrates that your choice of box will have a critical bearing on how your toilet is to be publicly perceived. Whatever design you carry, the aim is that it becomes a subtle conversation piece. Searching for boxes of more elaborate construction (such as the recent trend among the Parisian elite for exclusive coal carved boxes) will single you out from your companions in a most agreeable fashion.

So essential is it that a lady be seen with an elegant snuffbox, one should nevertheless be carried even by those unfortunate enough not to have acquired a taste for the practice. Indeed, with a little artful sleight of hand, the *appearance* of taking snuff may be given without the slightest grain of powder ever entering the nasal cavity.

Snuff is available scented with a variety of delicate oils. Choose according to your personal taste and preference. Lavender, bergamot, rose, cloves or jasmine all offer appropriately feminine perfumes.

The medicinal benefits of tobacco have long been celebrated, namely its ability to restore balance to the body following any excess of fluids. However, in some medical quarters, those benefits have most recently been called into question. Some individuals would have us believe that over-use of snuff can cause a young man to be unsteady in his gait, experience uncontrollable trembling of the hand and, worse, exhibit an unwelcome *wilting* of his dignity brought about by a much shrunk magnificence in the region of his noblest parts. Though this opinion is far from ubiquitous in medical circles, it may be worthy of some reflection on the part of all young ladies; particularly should you find yourself pursued by a snuffing suitor, able neither to walk with sound balance nor hold steady his hand…

How to Enjoy the Indian Weed with Propriety

INSPIRED BY THE EIGHTEENTH CENTURY ARISTOCRATIC
LOVE AFFAIR WITH TOBACCO

How to Wear a Bustle

'A HOMEMADE BUSTLE CANNOT BE SAT UPON WITHOUT
RISK OF DAMAGE, SO LADIES MUST BE DEMURE AND PUSH
THE CONSTRUCTION TO ONE SIDE, BALANCING CAREFULLY
UPON A SIDE PORTION OF POSTERIOR WHEN
ATTEMPTING TO SIT DOWN.'

Those of you with ambitions of rank and high fashion would be wise to take note of the remarkable toilet worn by ladies in every well-dressed circle. Even women of modest means should aspire to the charms of the bustled silhouette. It is a shape which speaks volumes of a lady's refinement, deportment and bearing. Indeed, as noted in a recent edition of that most esteemed publication, *Demorest's Magazine*:

> In reality, there is no figure that does not require, in the centre of the back, the addition of some narrow and projecting [bustle], which, gradually tapering out serves as a support to the drapery below.

How to Wear a Bustle

Demorest's Magazine further notes that without this bustle (or *tournure*, as is considered a more elegant term), 'there would be a falling in at the back, which would be very ungraceful, and in opposition to all present ideas'.

When adopting this most alluring of fashions, as you assuredly will, then you should take note of the following advice. The underskirt of your costume should be worn as flat as practicable at the front with all the fullness of the overskirt pulled rigorously to the back to form cascades of the most eye-catching folds. The whole ensemble should be supported by a foundation of whalebone or steel strips placed in the top back of the petticoat or by a separate construction tied around the waist. The bustle should be prominent, adding no breadth to the hips, but instead, pushing the heavy drapery of the skirts back as far as is comfortably possible. Your dress skirt should be trimmed with ruches, ribbons and fringes, but do not give in to the temptation to be overly elaborate. True elegance is to be found in the precision of cut rather than in the extravagance of ornament.

Bustles come in many shapes, sizes and materials. They can be manufactured at home, if you have a mind to it, from ruffles, wires, curved boning, pads or springs. A homemade bustle cannot be sat upon without risk of damage, so ladies must be demure and push the construction to one side, balancing carefully upon a side portion of posterior when attempting to sit down. Those who have the means to purchase a custom-made *collapsible* bustle will find it goes some way towards easing the predicament of how to sit. These marvellous inventions are so arranged with springs as to fold up whenever the wearer is sitting or lying down; the bustle resuming its proper position upon rising. Most ingenious!

Ladies concerned with matters of health would do well to purchase a scientific 'Braided Wire Health Bustle', which is recommended by physicians to be 'less heating to the spine than any others'.

Bustled dresses should be dark but faded in colour; full or vivid colours look far too fresh and vulgar, particularly when worn by women of mature years. Avoid at all costs comments made by those associated with the Rational Dress Movement. These unfortunate aesthetes are under the illusion that rigorous corseting, padding and boning is unhealthy and ugly! To advocate loose clothing, no corsets, bustles nor shoes with heels is surely to be misguided in the extreme! These unfortunates are to be scorned if the respect of society is to continue to shine upon you and your most divine toilet.

⚶

BASED ON THE HISTORY OF THE BUSTLE, A STYLE OF DRESS POPULAR IN THE EARLY 1870S AND REVIVED FOR A SHORT PERIOD IN THE MID-1880S. ADAPTED, IN PART, FROM AN ORIGINAL ARTICLE IN *DEMOREST'S MAGAZINE*, 1876

How to Manage a Newborn

'MANY WOMEN OF GENTLE SENSIBILITIES, WHO CONSIDER
THE SUCKLING OF THEIR NEWBORN TO BE UNFASHIONABLE
OR, INDEED, REPULSIVE, MAY CHOOSE TO FEED THEIR
INFANT UPON PAP.'

When a gentlewoman finds herself in the seasonable
condition of being with child, it is as well for her to
remember to take the utmost care of her own health for a
life of infinite delicacy will soon be dependent upon it.
There is scarcely any good reason why a new mother
should rise from her bed before six weeks is out. In some
classes of society there is an absurd notion that it is *clever*
for a woman to feel her feet as soon as is practicable after
giving birth, and that a new mother who rises quickly from
her bed is to be *envied* in some manner. This notion is
plainly ridiculous as a lengthy repose is certainly required
to ensure the future health and strength of the mother.

This period of bed rest is not necessary for country
women, of course; it is inconceivable that they should give

up work to take care of themselves. Indeed, it would be foolhardy and *injurious* for them to do so, as those inured to hard labour and exertion must not change their habits. It would be as harmful for the labourer's wife to give up her daily work for any period of time as for a lady, used to comfortable living, to take up cleaning her own house and cooking in her own kitchens! For health's sake, we must keep to what we are accustomed by nature.

A newborn should be put to the breast within three hours of emergence, and for the first month the suckling should be timed at intervals of an hour and a half. An efficient nurse will be capable of judging from the cries of a child whether it is hungry or experiencing some other discomfort, and will know when to present the child for feeding. If, for any unfortunate reason, a lady is ineffectual in nursing her child and unwilling or unable to secure the services of a wet nurse, then the most suitable substitute for mother's own nourishment is a quarter pint of fresh milk (from *one* cow) and warm water with a teaspoon of sugar dissolved therein. Many women of gentle sensibilities, who consider the suckling of their newborn to be unfashionable or, indeed, repulsive, may choose to feed their infant upon *pap*, a most nutritious substance made from crumbs of bread, water, milk and brown sugar. Milk or pap should always be served warm, as cold food is apt to give an infant wind which causes much torment to the mother.

A baby in pain should never be dosed with narcotics. Colic in the stomach can be remedied with a few drops of peppermint oil mixed with sweetened water and a hot flannel placed across the back.

It is common practice for a newborn to sleep with its nurse, although we hear there are some ladies who think it more natural to take their child to their own beds. Heaven forbid this fashion should catch on! There is nothing more ruinous to a lady's beauty than a disturbance of sleep!

A wise physician will advise that the most suitable place to house an infant during daylight hours is in a nursery situated in the upper part of a home, where the air circulates more freely and cleanly. The aspect of the nursery is of the greatest importance and if at all possible should be exposed to the south. A light, airy and sunny environment will ensure a well-trained child acquires a ruddy bloom, which speaks well of its parentage. Beware of housing your child in a gloomy and shadowy corner of the house: it will all too soon resemble the pallid and ill-fed population who are raised in the gutters of the city.

It is usual and agreeable practice for an infant to sleep in a cradle by the fire during the day. If the weather is particularly cold and inclement, a hot brick wrapped in a flannel may be placed at the infant's feet.

Once an infant reaches the age of nine months it is apt to become unhealthy and it is advisable then to bathe it in cold water several times a week. An infant should never be too delicately nurtured; it needs to grow accustomed to hardships in order that it may live a long and fruitful life.

How to Manage a Newborn

Irregular meals, hard and unforgiving beds, no pillows and a paucity of blankets are all to be encouraged.

The bodily wants of newborns are all too easy to satisfy and God will have blessed you as a woman with all the necessary talents, and staff, to fulfil your role as a loving and dedicated mother.

BASED ON ADVICE GIVEN IN *CASSELL'S HOUSEHOLD GUIDE*, C.1880S, AND OTHER CHILDCARE ADVICE FROM THE NINETEENTH CENTURY

How to Alight from a Carriage

'NO GENTLEMAN COMPANION SHOULD PRESUME TO SIT
NEXT TO YOU UNLESS HE IS INVITED TO DO SO ... HE SHOULD
ENSURE THE SKIRTS OF YOUR DRESS ARE PLACED IN SUCH
A MANNER AS TO AVOID BEING CRUSHED OR STEPPED UPON,
AND THAT YOUR KNEES ARE COVERED WITH A LAP ROBE.'

There can be no more healthful pursuit than to take a
drive in a well-appointed equipage. To sit well in a
carriage, with grace and poise, is an elegant accomplish-
ment most conducive to the well-being and demeanour of
the feminine frame. One's choice of carriage is much
dependent upon the change in fashions; more so than any
practical considerations which seem to dominate the
whims of gentlemen. A lady will choose her mode of
transport by its pleasing lines and décor, and *not* on its effi-
ciency and function.

The *Landau* is a most agreeable carriage to have at your
disposal, not least because it has a low shell, ensuring that
all occupants and their attire will be most visible. It is a
delightful occupation to disport oneself between the fash-

ionable hours of 5.30 and 7.30 on a warm and balmy evening upon the avenue of Rotten Row and the South Carriage Drive of Hyde Park. It is amusing to look upon the gentlemen *peacocking* in all their finery and to admire the fine mounts with their tails and manes tossing gaily on the breeze. It is of course with no small measure of satisfaction that you take note of the envy on the faces of all you pass.

You will have taken the utmost care with your toilet before embarking upon your evening's airing and will be attired in your richest and most brilliant of costumes. Your best satins and silks, and your most sumptuous wraps, should be displayed with the *highest* degree of elegance, befitting your elevated position in society and showing your beauty to its best advantage.

Driving in comfort and safety requires a high measure of feminine artistry and the rules governing deportment are laid down with consummate precision. When endeavouring to enter a carriage your driver should ensure the vehicle is stationed close to the kerbstone with the horses turned from it. The most courteous of drivers will see to it that the horses are calmed and will restrain them with his right hand whilst offering you his left. You must place your right foot upon the carriage step and, with the most delicate of hops, send yourself into the carriage.

It is your place to sit on the right hand of the seat facing the horses, indeed 'tis the place of honour and one you would only see fit to relinquish should you take a drive with a lady of higher ranking than your good self. No gentleman companion should presume to sit next to you unless he is invited to do so; a married lady's husband being the exception. A gentleman should wait until you are seated then enter the carriage with his back turned towards the seat he will occupy, so as to avoid any of the awkward stumbling which so often accompanies an attempt to turn around. He will, of course, have ensured the skirts of your dress are placed in such a manner as to avoid being crushed or stepped upon, that your knees are covered with a lap robe and that you are in possession of your fan, shawl, parasol and any other items pertinent to your comfort. Any disregard in these matters may offend your good reputation.

Your driver will proceed at a pace most comfortable to your composure, paying the utmost regard to your feminine sensibilities. If his driving is not to your taste, you must upon no account attempt to take the reins. Only ladies of an *hysterical* nature are prone to this action. A lack of serenity is much frowned upon and can only end in disaster.

Once all pleasure has been derived from the evening's excursion, and your driver has returned you to your place of residence, then you must proceed to alight from your carriage with as much grace and dignity as if you were under the expert observation of an empress. It is indeed an art to descend from a carriage with a flowing ease of elegance. The driver will open the doors and lower the steps and, if a gentleman has been present on the drive, then he will furnish you with his assistance. You may place your hands upon the gentleman's shoulders and he will place his hands gently underneath your elbows as you step neither hurriedly nor stiffly, but with calm assurance from the carriage to the ground. The gentleman will then see to it that your skirts are guarded from being soiled or muddied from the carriage wheels as this tedious occurrence can only spoil what has been a delightful and gratifying drive.

ADAPTED FROM *GASKELL'S COMPENDIUM OF FORMS, SOCIAL, EDUCATIONAL, LEGAL & COMMERCIAL,* 1880

How to Care for Your Oral Toilet

'WE HAVE RARELY KNOWN A LITTLE LAUDANUM-SOAKED
PIECE OF COTTON, CLENCHED BETWEEN THE TEETH, OR
ELSE A STICKING PLASTER THE BIGNESS OF A SIXPENCE,
FILLED WITH OPIUM AND AFFIXED TO THE TEMPORAL
ARTERY, FAIL TO EASE THE TOOTHACHE.'

There is nothing a young lady may do that she will thank herself more for in later life than to see to the proper care and maintenance of her oral toilet. The teeth are not only the jewels of the face, but are the instruments of mastication, a first and vital step in the process by which food is transported through the gut. No lady should risk the horror of the gentleman barber to render good bad teeth unless she is of a mind to do so. Would that we had the dental expertise of the French! Instead, we herein set out to be your guide that your oral toilet may be addressed in the comfort of your own boudoir.

A lady seeking guidance on the question of dentifrice creams and powders may well turn to advertisements in the newspapers. If so, she must proceed with caution!

Many of the creams secured via this means can cause untold damage, being comprised of substances such as brick dust or powdered earthenware pot, which are of such caustic nature as can strip off the enamel from the surface of your teeth and eat away at the gums. We would also caution you against overuse of dentifrice powders: applying them with a rough hand nightly will do more harm than good.

If the teeth and breath be rendered foul from a yellow covering, this can be remedied with the use of a thin strip of soft wood dipped into vinegar. This can be a lengthy process, if the teeth be so well covered as to hide their natural state, but your perseverance will be well rewarded by the end result.

We have it on good authority that officers of His Majesty's army apply a good covering of gunpowder, by way of the severed end of a chisel, on a fortnightly basis to the teeth. This, to very marked effect: the white smiles of many an officer cannot be faulted! Also favoured is a mouth rinse with human urine, which has a beneficial effect upon the teeth, though less so upon the sweetness of the breath. A lady of delicate persuasion may be forgiven for shunning such methods (although a tincture of myrrh will do well to hide the stench afterwards).

Ladies of gentle sensibilities should see to it that the mouth is rinsed after every meal with cold water, and that nightly application of a fine powder of two parts chalk, one part Peruvian bark and one of hard soap is applied gently with a soft brush. The addition of a little borax will create a pleasantly foaming effect which assists well in the process. This routine acts agreeably upon both teeth and gums, and will not have an abrasive impact upon either.

It can happen that some knock – for example, from the hoof of a horse, or from the untimely opening of a carriage door – can dislodge a tooth from its secure bedding in the gum. Fear not! Should such an unfortunate incident occur, it need not blight your day. See that you locate the tooth and have a trusted maidservant replace it in the socket, fixing it thence with fine cat gut or with the Indian weed. In time, it will re-root itself with a satisfactory sureness.

The only remedy for teeth that have been loosened by the poor health of the gums, which can become overly soft following the scurvy, is that the gums be regularly split open and bled generously. Only then will they have a chance of gaining in strength. A mouthwash with a cold water tincture of bark will speed the healing process.

There can be nothing more tiresome than the pain of a troubled tooth! The humours must be drawn off from the gums surrounding the affected area. Leeches, when applied to the gum, are especially effective here. Promote perspiration, too: bathe the feet in warm water and take a drink of dilute wine-whey frequently. Purging and inducing vomits are often exceedingly beneficial in calming a toothache. Often this readjustment of the humours will be all that is required to ease the pain.

If the pain persists and can be located to its source (that source being a hollow tooth carved out by decay whereby the nerve is exposed), then a trusted friend, with steady hand and a steadier nerve, may greatly ease the condition if they apply the merest drop of creosote to the cavity by way of a darning needle. This will seal off the nerve and, similarly, the pain. But extreme caution should be employed: should the creosote spill, it will act corrosively upon the flesh of the mouth. Furthermore, hold a bag filled with the flowers of camomile or elder, which have been boiled, alongside the troublesome tooth, or else a toasted fig. These will promote the subsiding of the inflammation, provided the heat thereof be as great as can be borne.

Failing all else, we have rarely known a little laudanum-soaked piece of cotton, clenched between the teeth, or else a sticking plaster the bigness of a sixpence, filled with opium and affixed to the temporal artery, fail to ease the toothache.

❦

ADAPTED FROM ORIGINAL DENTAL ADVICE IN HOUSEHOLD MANUALS, SUCH AS *THE HOUSEHOLD CYCLOPEDIA OF GENERAL INFORMATION* BY THOMAS KELLY, 1881, AND DR W. BUCHAN'S *DOMESTIC MEDICINE*, 1785

How to Defend Your Home Against Evil Curses

'A WITCH MAY HAVE THE POWER OF MAGIC ON HER
SIDE, BUT THERE IS SOME COMFORT IN THE FACT THAT
A HAG IS DECIDEDLY ILL-EDUCATED, AND AS SUCH MAY
BE EASILY MISLED.'

Any lady of strict Christian upbringing must surely abhor the practice of countering the vexations of a troublesome acquaintance by the laying down of a curse. Not only does such an exercise invoke the wrath of the Lord, it will moreover *wreak havoc* with one's reputation (and, henceforth, one's marriage potential). That much notwithstanding, it has been known that ladies, even those of some considerable social standing, will adopt such an extreme and ill-advised course when confronted by an individual so troublesome as to leave little room for alternative measures. In such circumstances, as has been told, one may call upon the assistance of the custodian of a Holy Well, examples of which may be sought out in most parishes. The ritual involves inscribing the name of the one that is to be cursed on paper, before tossing it into the waters. Then the individual must thrice drink from the well, whereupon illness and misfortune of the most incapacitating nature will thereafter be visited on the victim.

Naturally, we do not wish to recommend so indecorous a course of action to any young lady (though we have heard tell that the well of St Eilan, on the isle of Anglesey, has the power to lay down curses of considerable potency). However, it is worthy of mention simply as a means of *counter*-action. One should seek protection from the unspeakable eventuality that one's household falls victim to such a curse. In this event, you may be sure that it is the power of *witchery* that has transported the evil into your home, where it will prey upon your health, wealth and sanity.

A witch may have the power of magic on her side, but there is some comfort in the fact that a hag is decidedly ill-educated, and as such may be easily misled. A well-worn shoe will bear the scent and imprint of the wearer in a way that no other garment can do. When it is concealed in the chimney stack, or within the wall above a doorway (both of which are the weakest spots for a household's defences against all things spiritually unwelcome), the witch will be duped into believing that there lies the subject of her curse, and thus all the magic will be expended upon the shoe, leaving the individual safe and unharmed. In the unlikely event that the witch is of sound enough intellect to detect that it is merely a decoy, rather than the individual in person, it will already be too late for her to rectify her mistake. Her journey down the chimney stack will have left her in a spot too tight to turn around to flee, and everyone knows that witches cannot travel backwards.

If you seek further insurance against evil, a witch's bottle will provide the ultimate defence. The glass or earthenware flask is bulbous and bladder-shaped. Fill it with anything sharp in nature: thorns, coarse grasses, coffin nails, pins and needles. Discreetly request that the gentleman of the house relieve his bladder into the bottle (not in such a surging torrent as would fill it, rather with the merest spray such as will provide a distinctly human scent). Top the bottle up with vinegar or wine, and seal it with a cork. Boil the contents over the fire for a few moments before concealing it within the chimney stack, along with the shoe.

The witch's magic, upon encountering the bottle, will turn upon herself, causing her an excruciating and burning pain in the bladder. Your genteel, feminine sensitivities may shudder at the prospect of inflicting such discomfort on another, but you may console yourself that your actions may well secure the salvation of her soul for all eternity. Her pain may be sufficient to enlighten her as to the error of her ways, and she may, in due course, be persuaded to adopt a more Christian lifestyle.

Finally, it is essential that such concealments remain

buried: not only within the fabric of your house, but also buried from public discussion. Whilst it is a wise woman who takes all necessary measures to protect herself from evil, it will not do to discuss such matters in polite company, lest the wrong impression be given out, and your reputation slighted. Besides, making public the whereabouts of such middens may serve to weaken the impact of the protection they aim to provide.

INSPIRED BY SUBSTANTIAL ARCHAEOLOGICAL EVIDENCE FROM EIGHTEENTH CENTURY BRITISH AND COLONIAL HOUSES

How to Choose a Wet Nurse

'A WELL-APPOINTED WET NURSE SHOULD HAVE ... GLOBES
OF A GOOD SIZE, NEITHER TOO FIRM, NOR TOO HANGING,
WITH PROTRUDING, EASY-TO-SUCKLE NIPS, WHICH SHOULD
GLOW WITH THE COLOUR OF FRESH STRAWBERRIES.'

A lady of high birth should shun the distasteful practice of suckling a newborn. It is a habit that women of the lower classes are wont to indulge in and one in which they have become most efficient. It is fortunate that this is so: should you wish your child to be nourished by the milk of Grace, then a willing wench with founts of nature fit to burst can, with due care and diligence, be found to nurture your offspring.

There are many things to be considered in the choosing of a wet nurse for your child. You must look closely to each candidate and base your final election on the respectability of their background and parentage, their age and fairness, their conduct and demeanour, their education, the excellence of their milk and the healthfulness of their own children.

How to Choose a Wet Nurse

Your chosen wet nurse must come from an unblemished background where no parent, grandparent nor great-grandparent was ever tainted by the stain of a bodily or mental deformity. She should be between the ages of 25 and 35 years, this being the time of life when most women are at their most healthful and hardy. She should be neither too big nor too small, and neither too portly nor too lean. Indeed, she should have a good covering of flesh on her arms and legs, but not trembling flesh: it should be firm and hard. She should not be squinty-eyed or lame, have crooked shoulders, a humped back, nor indeed any hint of deformity. She should have a clear and unsullied complexion with neither blemishes nor spots. She should most certainly not be encumbered by tresses of a reddish hue (a mid-chestnut brown would be the ideal).

She should have a comely face, a straight nose, a ruddy mouth and white teeth. She should not smell. Her globes should be of a good size, neither too firm, nor too hanging, with protruding, easy-to-suckle nips, which should glow with the colour of fresh strawberries. She should not drink wine nor indulge in greediness. She should be merry and good-humoured at all times, willing to sing and play with your child, and to offer it sustenance whenever it so desires. She should not be with child herself, nor should she partake in rapturous relations with her husband or any other man. Such actions will render her secretions stale and of little worth.

Her milk should be of the highest quality and neither

too watery nor too thick. It should be of the purest white, with neither a bluish or yellowy hue. It should have a sweet and palatable flavour, and any wet nurse whose milk tastes sour, sharp or bitter should not be considered, as she is sure to be possessed of a mealy mouth and a melancholic nature which could prove most injurious to the health of your child.

A sure way to test the quality of a nurse's milk is to bid her to release some on to a shiny surface such as a looking glass. If, when the glass is tilted, the milk flows quickly and separates, then it is too watery. And if the milk flows sluggishly, then it is too thick and full of fat. A flow betwixt the two would be most ideal.

A well-appointed nurse should spill freely and abundantly so that your child should never have to suckle her breasts dry; indeed, a glut of nature's nectar can prove most beneficial when rubbed on pimples, or used to cool an itching rash. If your child should wet in its crib immediately upon feeding, then you can be sure your nurse has an ample supply. Beware, though, the nurse who would seek to deceive you by feeding your child water in secret, or one who herself wets in your child's bed. A creature of such heinous nature should be run from your home with a whip!

Any child of a wet nurse should be older than two months, but younger than eight months when she first enters your employ. You can then be certain her milk is neither too new, nor too stale. If her own child is a boy then you can be assured that the milk will be of a superior quality than if her child was a girl. If you take care to refer to these recommendations then you may be assured that a well-nourished child will be yours and the perfect swell and firmness of your own *décolletage* will continue to be much admired.

BASED ON *THE HAPPY DELIVERIE OF WOMEN* BY
JAMES GUILLEMEAU, 1612

How to be an Obedient Wife

'THE IDEAL WIFE ... SHOULD BLUSH EASILY, EXHIBIT
MODESTY IN EVERYTHING, AND SUBMIT TO HER
HUSBAND IN ALL THINGS.'

Marriage *for love* is a current curiosity of mode, and we intend herein to cast any thoughts of such folly far from the minds of the judicious woman. This fast-growing tendency among gentlewomen causes so much instability, as, in the process of pursuing their 'love', many reject the necessity of seeking a marriage contract with a gentleman of at least equal title.

God's primary purpose for the sacred institution of marriage is surely to protect the most holy rank and order of society which He, in His wisdom, has beseeched us to consent to with serenity, for the sake of the beauty of His world. Constancy and uniformity is essential for the good of God's people. Any reasonable woman may be certain of lasting happiness so long as she may be in receipt of that which is necessary to *maintain* her condition. That is to say, so long as she can live at least in the manner in which her mother lived, she may content herself.

Marriage is the means by which a woman may secure her own and her family's rightful place in such a Divine Order. All that is required of a single gentlewoman is that she applies a careful scrutiny to the character and Christian values of her suitor prior to responding to his offer of marriage. This will assure her of a marriage that is not only fiscally profitable, but also provides a tolerable and lifelong friendship. Romantic love is a mere transient distraction from the real business of marriage.

If *natural* circumstances were to result in our being brought low in title, then it is only right and fitting that we thereafter accept God's Will with thanks. This notwithstanding, it is not for us to *undo* that which He has ordained by *wilfully* seeking to degrade ourselves in a marriage beneath our station. To do so would be to demonstrate the very basest manners to Heaven itself: for if one is blessed with a happy lot in life, one is thereby granted all the more time with which to prepare oneself for the next, by way of quiet contemplation and the carrying out of good works to the benefit of those less blessed. Who are we, that we may so propel ourselves into wretched drudgery for the sake of a 'love' contract with one beneath us?

Beware the unfortunate circumstances that befall those women who find themselves so misled by the courtship of a lesser-ranking man that they condescend to a clandestine marriage. Such a contract is entered into without the eyes of God, in the presence of only two mortal witnesses. Any lady of estimable upbringing will naturally assume that the 'marriage' is none the less binding. Such men as entice a lady so (titillated, no doubt, by the richness of her beauty and, moreover, of her family's estate), do not recognise such bonds. And when the lady's family withdraw both dowry and inheritance, as they are rightly justified in so doing, these depraved men of the lesser classes will often desert their feeble contract, leaving the woman vulnerable and desolate, and her offspring bastard.

There is another trend of greater distress to us: that of a woman snubbing her sacred vow to *obey* her husband. We acknowledge that there is nothing quite so disagreeable as the wife who finds herself burdened for life with a man of tyrannical nature, despicable temper and ignorant wit. A husband who labours his right to be obeyed in all things ungracious and imprudent is a cross that is hard for any woman to bear.

But bear it she must! For it is only with a submissive and subservient deportment that a wife may learn to surrender herself to God's Will. Her husband may be a surly old dotard, whose splenetic morosities may make her life unpleasant, but if she react to this with impropriety, 'tis she alone that will bring about the ruin of her reputation. In truth, she who dances must sooner or later pay the piper! Conversely, should she choose to bear in private the shortcomings of her husband, without so much as a whisper to even her closest confidante, she maintains complete respectability.

Let us not overlook the fact that, for every woman, marriage is full of inconveniences. (Is there any condition in a woman's life that is without them?) A marriage must not become a battle for supremacy! It is a wife's *obligation* to obey, just as it is a husband's *duty* to respect. How can it become a lady to rebuke her Christian responsibilities, simply because her husband has turned his back on his?

The ideal wife must see to it that her appearance is befitting of her station, though without giving out that her appearance is a matter of any importance. She should blush easily, exhibit modesty in everything, and submit to her husband in all things. Let her actions speak louder and ring truer than any words. Her very virtue and Christianity will hold a mirror to any unreasonable demands her husband may make of her, without the need for her to declare her independence in any respect.

Therefore we urge wives to heed our counsel: *do not succumb to contention!*

It is your duty to show a modest and retiring character, a placid temper, patience and composure in all things. Resist conceit, din, bile, displeasure and agitation. Return your husband's disrespect with nothing more than a faint reproach; your feminine composure will cut him far deeper than any raucous lashing of the tongue may do.

ADAPTED FROM *SOME REFLECTIONS UPON MARRIAGE*
BY MARY ASTELL, 1700

How to Preserve Your Looks

'NEVER ADVERTISE YOUR USE OF COSMETICS; IT IS
UNDIGNIFIED AND, INDEED, SOME WOULD SAY SCANDALOUS,
TO SHOW ANY WEAKNESS FOR LIP OR CHEEK ROUGE.'

I t is much frowned upon for a lady of gentility to be in
possession of anything other than the palest of complexions
(a soft translucency akin to the petals of the most delicate and
fragile of flowers). Indeed, any mark of sun or weather upon
the skin looks vulgar, coarse and most unbecoming. A gentlewoman, intent upon preserving her looks, should not
venture outside the front door without the protection of her
parasol; indeed, she should avoid taking the air at all during
the heat of the summer months and should confine herself to
the coolness of her parlour. The rays of the sun can prove
harmful even when indoors and it would be prudent to keep
the drapes drawn tight at all times.

Although dreadful indeed for the sufferer, the effect of
consumption upon one's appearance is most becoming
and fashionable. A white lead skin powder and a little
rouge applied discreetly to the cheeks will imitate the
desirable aspects of this illness most satisfactorily. Ladies

who covet the bright eyes of the disease may rinse their own eyes in a little lemon juice or belladonna to bring about the prettiest of sparkles.

Most ladies will agree that a most charming degree of paleness can be induced by simply drinking a little vinegar and avoiding the fresh air. Consumed in small quantities, chalk and iodine can also bring about a most pleasing pallor. A lady's *décolletage* is her prime feature and many a marriage has been determined by its condition. Every effort should be made to preserve the softness and vulnerability, and the painting on of fine blue lines will help to increase the appearance of delicate transparency.

Many society hostesses, upon reaching middle age, may find their complexions far from radiant; indeed, those who spend the majority of their leisure entertaining in the polluted atmosphere of town, and who have dined to excess on a rich diet, may find their complexions to be completely ravaged. This is the time in many a gentlewoman's life when the mere pinching of cheeks and biting of lips proves useless in execution. Although we would *never* recommend the overuse of any form of artificial make-up (we would not wish *you* to be associated with the unsavoury ladies of the theatre), it has come to our notice that a certain Mrs Henning operates a beauty salon in South Molton Street, where she will welcome any ladies of good standing through a discreet back door. It is recommended you go heavily veiled and alight quickly from your carriage to avoid any undue recognition and subsequent embarrassment.

How to Preserve Your Looks

Mrs Henning may prove to be a great help in preserving the myth of your natural beauty, particularly in the eyes of your husband. All too often the naivety of men leads them to believe a woman's beauty is *bestowed* by Mother Nature, and who would wish to deliver them from this innocent misconception? *Never* advertise your use of cosmetics; it is undignified and, indeed, some would say scandalous, to show any weakness for lip or cheek rouge. We do believe, however, that *papier poudre* (those splendid little books of coloured paper) can help remove shine and will leave a faint trace of colour when pressed to cheeks or nose. A burnt matchstick will provide a darkening of the eyelashes where Nature left too delicate a touch, and geranium and poppy petals leave a most comely stain upon the lips.

Women who have reached a certain age, and whose complexions resist any artificial assistance, may wish to try sleeping with strips of raw beef bound around their faces. This is said to be remarkable for reducing wrinkles.

Above all, a lady must keep a sweet and serene expression, avoiding extravagant laughter and unnecessary distortions of the mouth when speaking. Ugly and discontented thoughts will age your countenance immeasurably and will be the cause of infinite regret.

BASED ON THE HISTORY OF COSMETICS FROM THE NINETEENTH CENTURY

How to Read the Man by Reading His Body

'IT IS IN THE THRUST AND POSTURE OF HIS CHEST, AND
THE SQUARE UPLIFT OF THE SHOULDERS THAT YOU SEE
EVIDENT HIS DEGREE AND QUANTITY OF MANHOOD.'

Any modern lady must equip herself to function to her best degree by keeping fully abreast of science. The most current scientific developments of spiritualism and mesmerism have unlocked the mysterious worlds of the after-life and of the innermost workings of the brain. Indeed, even Her Most Gracious Majesty has attended séances and consulted with a medium. But for its practical implications upon daily life, it is with the science of phrenology that a lady should pay her most studious attentions.

The science of phrenology has its origins in Alpine Europe, with the work of Dr Gall of Vienna, and Dr Lavater of Switzerland, who first noted the correlation between the nature and talents of a person, and their facial construction and characteristics. Indeed, Dr Lavater's observations extended to the most enlightening findings on the effect of a good death upon the human countenance: that several days after passing over, the features of the face become more aligned and harmonised, having the effect of making a person *more beautiful in death*. But in England it has been the work and genius of Dr George Combe that has raised phrenology up to its most respectable and meaningful level. For he has made clear the means by which it may be utilised to assess the character of a man.

Phrenology informs us that each function of the brain is located in a different division of the skull. When that function is called upon to perform in a person, it will pull the head into line with its cerebral location. Herein lies the most useful method of assessing what it is that truly lies behind a person's words: if a man passes the time making polite trivialities of conversation with you, you may nevertheless gauge the key to his innermost sensibilities. Ladies, make note! For, if it is his *love* for you that presides over his brain, you will see it made evident in his head, as it tilts gently backwards, as the love function of the brain is located in the lower, rear division of the skull. When love is called upon by the subconscious mind to perform, it pulls the head back, as it does during the act of embracing.

You may wish to ascertain the nature of a man ever before you make his proper acquaintance. In this case, a little scientific knowledge will also be of invaluable assistance. Look to his chest, for it is in the thrust and posture of the chest, and the square uplift of the shoulders that you see evident his *degree* and *quantity* of manhood. A well-sexed man will stand erect, with his chest up and proud, his shoulders back. Reject the man whose stance and gait is older than his years, for it is certain his amount of gender is lacking.

Furthermore, you will assess his degree of passion quite effectively, and ever before your wedding night, if you look to the plunge and thrust of his hips during the act of laughter. If you should utter something of amusement in his company, observe how the love function of his brain will pull back his head, whilst his lower body is thrust forward, from the hips, in the direction of your own pelvis. Nature thus makes ready for the assigning of his seed, and thereby illustrates to you the extent of his desire and sensuality so to do.

How to Read the Man by Reading His Body

By comparison, observe how he laughs in the presence of, for example, his dear Mama, or the Reverend's wife. If you are to experience a joyful wedding night, you will see the *lacking* of his desire, clearly present in his laughter there. This will leave you in no doubt as to his degree of passion for you.

ADAPTED FROM *PRIVATE LECTURES ON PERFECT MEN, WOMEN AND CHILDREN* BY PROFESSOR O. S. FOWLER, 1880

How to Kill, Cook and Serve
a Sea-Turtle

'THERE IS NOTHING MORE ALLURING THAN SERVING FARE
THAT CANNOT BE HUNTED ON THE GROUNDS OF YOUR
COUNTRY ESTATE, NOR CULLED FROM YOUR FARMLANDS.'

From the kitchens of the vast plantation houses of the West Indies, we have learned of such exotic delights as have hitherto never been dreamt of. It is currently possible to procure the gastronomic fare of the far seas for yourself to savour at your own table and dumbfound your guests. Of all the delicacies to reach our shores, by far the most sought-after in gentle circles is the great sea-turtle. The creatures are transported across the oceans in barrels of sea water; a carriage that suits them well as they are thereby kept alive a great while. The sweetest of all varieties is the green turtle, so-called because of its delectable green fat. On the palate it resembles something of a meeting of lobster and veal.

How to Kill, Cook and Serve a Sea-Turtle

Turtle soup has become highly fashionable in England in recent years; so much so, that certain taverns in Covent Garden keep several dozen live turtles at any one time, in order that any party desirous of turtle soup may be so obliged. We herein lay down instructions whereby you may direct your cook in the fine art of killing, cooking and presenting a sea-turtle in your own home. Doubt not that it will result in gasps of appreciation from the most exacting of dinner-guest, and will leave them speaking of you as a hostess of the very highest calibre for days to follow.

One large creature will be sufficient for a party of two dozen to dine quite adequately. You will need to have your man procure a live turtle, as by this means you may best ascertain its freshness.

Preparing Your Turtle for Cooking

Firstly, your turtle will need to be immersed in boiling water, deep enough that the back and belly, head and fins may be thoroughly scalded. Thereafter, and by seven in the morning, suspend the creature by the hind fins and remove its head, placing a vessel beneath with which to retain the blood for stock.

Dressing the Turtle Limbs

After a period of 12 hours or so, cut down the turtle. Remove fins, head and tail, and throw them into simmering salted water for several hours. Remove them from the water at the point at which they begin to give under the pressure of your knife. Then add salt and pepper, and place directly on to the searing heat of the fire, so as to avoid rendering giblets laboursome and tough. Thereafter, put the seared parts into a pot, along with a selection of fragrant vegetables such as onion, celery and leek. Add some sweet spices and a tied bunch of thyme, marjoram and parsley. Make a thick liquor sauce with sweet white wine, sherry, water, lemon or lime juice, the blood-stock and a thickener. When the sauce is done, pour it into the pot. This makes a most delicate dish to accompany turtle pie or roast turtle.

Spit-Roasting the Turtle Flesh

Remove a hunk of flesh from the body of the turtle, and scrape out and clean the outer shell in which you will present the finished dish.

Prick the flesh all over with cloves and drench in a liquor of lemon juice, fine lemon rind and sweet white wine. Affix it to the spit, and baste it periodically with more of the lemon liquor. As it cooks, dust with flour and crumbed bread, and douse with butter from time to time until it has an appetising appearance. Then, take the greenish fat that has collected in the pan beneath the spit and cook it off fast with more sweet white wine, sherry, lemon peel, salt and sugar. Serve the flesh, diced into cubes and drenched with these hot juices, delicately arranged in the polished upper shell, tastefully garnished with sprigs of sweet herbs and any other exotic produce as you have been able to acquire.

There is nothing more alluring than serving fare that cannot be hunted on the grounds of your country estate, nor culled from your farmlands. Livestock and game are not without their own peculiar delights, but do not compete with a dish of so lavish a provenance.

INSPIRED BY THE VOGUE FOR TURTLE-EATING IN RESPECTABLE EIGHTEENTH CENTURY ENGLISH SOCIETY AND ADAPTED FROM AN ORIGINAL RECIPE IN RICHARD BRADLEY'S COUNTRY HOUSEWIFE AND LADY'S DIRECTOR, PART TWO, 1732

How to Receive Callers

'WE HEARTILY RECOMMEND A BRIEF PIANO DUET; NOTHING
WILL PROVIDE YOU WITH A MORE SATISFYING OPPORTUNITY
TO ENJOY A CLOSE PHYSICAL PROXIMITY TO YOU BEAU.'

If she is to uphold her position within society, any lady of breeding must set aside a day for calling. It is vital that strict codes be applied to the receiving of all callers.

Firstly, ensure that a small table, placed near the main doorway to your home, displays a silver calling-card tray, with up-turned 'pie-crust' edges so as to prevent the cards falling. Your servant should place all received cards upon the tray and present it to you on the upturned palm of her left hand. From this safe vantage you may assess your callers: any who have called in person, whom you are not of an inclination to receive, will simply be informed by your servant that you are 'not at home'. Reject all who do not observe the correct hours of calling unless they have the advantage of age. Resist, too, any temptation to respond that you 'beg to be excused'; it is a most impolite and unseemly formula.

Upon receiving a first call from one new to your neighbourhood, you are wise to receive only the card, not the caller in person, until such time as you have ascertained their suitability and sought out their reputation. Be sure that you, and any daughters receiving with you, are appropriately attired in morning wear. Never bring a favourite dog into the drawing-room with you to receive; the horror of its dusty feet or its over-familiarity infringing on the skirts of your lady guests is to be avoided at all costs.

Informal morning calls are always made more cheery by offering tea with a selection of cakes. If you are receiving calls on New Year's Day, you may wish to offer a beverage of an intoxicating nature, though you would be wise to limit the quantity thereof; gentleman callers on this day will almost certainly have a number of calls to make and will undoubtedly be offered a tipple at each. Inebriation is never acceptable; far be it from you to be party to such embarrassment.

If your callers are agreeable to you, you should instruct your servant to usher them into the drawing-room, made inviting in anticipation with floral displays of a modest nature, and a fire, if the air has a chill. Stand upon their arrival in the room. During the visit it is not customary for you to retain a servant in the room.

A lady should always be offered the seat closest in proximity to yours, whereas a gentleman must always be left to find his own seat. Never presume to accommodate a gentleman's hat or gloves; he should see to his hat himself, and it is, in any case, bad form for him to dispose of his gloves unless he is of intimate acquaintance. His visit must take up no longer than 20 minutes of your time, 30 in the most extreme of cases; he should retain hat and gloves in his hands in respect of this.

When your guest stands to leave, you should rise too, and may offer your caller your hand, if you so wish. Accompany male or female callers to the door of the drawing-room only. The only circumstance in which you should walk them to the door of your home is if the age of the caller gives them the advantage.

See that your conversation is befitting of a lady. One should avoid anything that may provoke discouraging remarks. Any contention that could be deemed to constitute a criticism of a religious or political nature should not be aired in your drawing-room. Steer clear, too, of the repetition of scandal, or the discussion of anyone, or anything, of questionable characteristics, for this betrays ill-breeding. Your manner of conversation, in addition to the subject thereof, should be guarded. A lady pitches her voice at an agreeable level, shunning boisterous mannerisms and the murmur alike.

If you are receiving a visit from a gentleman with whom you are courting, propriety dictates that you retain your dignity, and therefore your distance, at all times. This notwithstanding, it is Nature's way that any young beau will be desirous of the *frisson* of his hand brushing against yours. Perhaps he will even long to sit close enough to you for your thighs to press gently together; in such a manner will you both be provided with an all too brief glimpse of the rapture of marriage. The challenge is how such intimacies may be engineered in the parlour without fear of reproof. To this effect we heartily recommend a brief piano duet; nothing will provide you with a more satisfying opportunity to enjoy a close physical proximity to your beau, all the while maintaining a rigorous respectability.

ADAPTED FROM ORIGINAL ADVICE IN *GOULD'S BLUE BOOK FOR THE CITY OF ST LOUIS, VOL. IV, 1886; A HANDBOOK OF ETIQUETTE FOR LADIES AND GENTLEMEN*, JAMES HOGG & SONS, LONDON, 1859, AND OTHER VICTORIAN ETIQUETTE MANUALS

How to Maintain a Most Comely Perruque

'IT SEEMS ALWAYS TO BEFALL A WOMAN TO HAVE TO CARRY WITH HER THE BURDEN OF TRUE BEAUTY. AS EVE WAS TO DISCOVER IN THE GARDEN OF EDEN, FOR EVERY PLEASURE WE MUST PAY A PRICE.'

It is a grotesque and unpardonable offence for a lady to be seen in public without her immaculately dressed and impeccably maintained wig. Indeed, it is every lady's ambition for her *perruque* to be the talk of the town. It is a blessing, then, that fashion should dictate the wearing of the most elaborate of wigs, for what lady has the time or inclination to keep her natural hair in a state of cleanliness? It is most unhealthy to bathe too often (it can only encourage the most fatal of illnesses), so it is most convenient to cover the hair in this manner and keep the lice in darkness. It is the French whom we must thank for this most liberating of fashions: in matters of taste, style and hygiene they are indeed unrivalled.

One must engage a wigmaker of wit and ambition whose great skills allow him to raise the height of every new creation; one whose hot clay pipes curl hanging chignons to perfection and one who can offer you an appearance of demure fairness, or serene and blissful charm. He must be the most discreet of gentlemen, one whom you can trust with your very modesty; he will, after all, be the only soul on earth to witness you in all your bare-headed innocence.

The most prized of wigs are woven from the hair of humans, but if you are burdened with difficulties of a pecuniary nature, then there is no shame in instructing your wigmaker to use horse or even goat hair. You must order the most flamboyant of styles; only when you are prevented from entering a room by the towering tallness arranged elegantly upon your head, should you let the sainted man rest and reward him for his efforts.

It will delight the senses of all who surround you if you endeavour to dress your wig to further increase its enormous size. Ringlets and curls of ample proportion, plumes of exotic feathers, platters of fruit, sweet songbirds in cages and galleon ships, with full sails aloft, are exquisite additions to your magnificent structure and will propel any lady of proper ambition to the very pinnacle of high society. 'Tis a noble woman indeed whose wig knocks at the very doors of heaven!

It seems always to befall a woman to have to carry with her the burden of true beauty. As Eve was to discover in the Garden of Eden, for every pleasure we must pay a price. So it is that you must bear with grace and fortitude the great weight of your wigmaker's art: the persistent pains in your head, and the great ache upon your shoulders, should be looked upon as mere inconveniences. Your discomfort should in no respect be permitted to diminish your stature or style.

The delicate structure and great elevation of your wig require that much forethought be taken when travelling about town or attending to the pleasures of society. Many a lady of less than graceful means has found herself in all manner of difficulties when entering or alighting from a carriage, and who has not heard the tales of ladies shamed to their graves after catching their coiffures alight on the hanging chandeliers of a ballroom?

Your night-time arrangements should allow you to sleep in an upright position to guard against any ruffling or damage to your wig. It is most pleasurable, at the end of a tiresome day, to rest your neck against a soft and billowing pillow, and to enjoy the delights afforded by a long-handled lice scratcher, which can relieve your itching at no cost to your curls. It is most unfortunate that mice are attracted to the animal grease so necessary in keeping your wig intact. If your proud coiffure should attract a family of the beastly vermin and their scampering and private habits become intolerable, then you must have your wigmaker remove your structure for a meticulous airing.

It is most comely and in keeping with a vision of ageless

beauty that you wear your wig white. To keep the whiteness pure and the stench of grease and mustiness at bay, it is requisite that it be powdered and scented daily. There are plentiful pomades to choose from which will impart a fruity freshness to your arrangement and many scents which may discourage the more persistent of small beasts. Retire to your powder room and have your maidservant cover your dress in a quantity of cloth and your face with a shield of glass, then let her proceed to dust your ensemble with just the correct amount of powder. It is wise that you instruct your maidservant correctly in this matter; a lady who is *over*powdered and leaves a trail of dust in her wake is apt to attract the attention of nought but ridicule.

BASED ON THE GEORGIAN WIG VANITY OF THE
EIGHTEENTH CENTURY

How to Ride Side-Saddle with Consummate Elegance

'NEVER CONSIDER MOUNTING A STEED, NO MATTER
HOW URGENTLY YOU ARE DESIROUS OF A RIDE, NOR HOW
HANDSOME THE SPECIMEN, UNLESS HE IS EQUIPPED
WITH THREE POMMELS.'

Gone are the days when a lady must succumb to the untold indelicacies of riding astride in the masculine fashion. No longer must she don split skirts to accomodate that ghastly imposition. A lady's anatomy is simply not designed to fit upon a horse's back thus: the rounded hunkers of her thighs will not comfortably permit it. No, the gracious equestrienne must give thanks to the side-saddle and the divine genius of whomsoever first patented the Leaping Head, which currently permits proprietous, and yet safe and controlled horsemanship for ladies. Never consider mounting a steed, no matter how urgently you are desirous of a ride, nor how handsome the specimen, without he is equipped with three pommels.

How to Ride Side-Saddle with Consummate Elegance

A lady may be assured that riding is a most elegant means of exercise, lending vitality, poise and good health to one's person. But it is an art which must be practised a good deal, if it is to be executed without blunder or derisory deportment. Whilst nothing can be expected to replace the tutelage of an expert trainer, we herein set down for your convenience a few pertinent pointers.

Firstly, see to it that your toilet is that which befits your horseback promenade. The billowing skirts of our mothers are no longer acceptable. Take your lead from European royal households, where riding habits are so slender and elongated that it is said some are sewn into them daily to enable a most elegant ride. A dark coloured cloth would suit, and it would be best paired with a coat buttoned high up the *décolletage* and tailed at the rear. Your corset, too, will need to be looked to: a higher cut will allow greater comfort and range of movement when in the saddle.

A satisfactory mounting requires that you call upon the assistance of both a groom and a gentleman escort. With the groom holding steady the animal's head, stand alongside the horse on its near side in the direction of the head. Have the escort face you directly, supporting your foot in his left hand. From this position, having gathered up your skirts in your left hand, grip the pommel of the saddle with your right. With as much delicacy and grace of movement as you can muster, spring lightly upwards, whereupon your gentleman escort will mirror this action with his supporting hand, having the effect of rendering you aloft and into the saddle. Your right knee should hook itself around the high pommel for your safety. The Leaping Head will then curve across your upper leg for your full protection. It is incumbent upon the gentleman now to locate the stirrup for you, and to position your skirts to your liking. See to it that your posture is fully erect and your torso forward facing at all times. With your hat well secured, a small, delicately carved, ivory-handled whip will complete your ensemble.

Bear in mind the old adage that, 'If you go left, you are sure to go right; and if you go right, you go wrong'! Which is to say, pass by oncoming riders always by the left. Your gentleman escort should ride at your side, unless he sees fit to ride ahead for matters pertaining to your greater comfort or safety. You may expect him not to pause to converse with any passers-by with whom he has made previous acquaintance; his duties lie in devoting his full and constant attentions to you.

You may take it on trust that your escort is well-practised enough at his horsemanship so as to have secured for you a horse that is seasoned in its experience of ladies riding side-saddle. The billow and rustle of skirts, and the placement of the rider in an unaccustomed position is too taxing for a novice horse and it should not befall you to enlighten the creature unless you are inclined so to do. If you entertain any doubts as to your gentleman's expertise in this respect, you may do well to consider seeking one more suitable: the gratification derived from a pleasurable ride will be thoroughly marred by an unskilful escort.

ADAPTED FROM ORIGINAL ADVICE IN *GASKELL'S COMPENDIUM OF FORMS, SOCIAL, EDUCATIONAL, LEGAL & COMMERCIAL,* 1880

How to Raise
Well-Mannered Children

'DO NOT GIVE IN TO FEELINGS OF EXCESSIVE FONDNESS
NOR SHOWER UPON YOUR CHILD ALL THAT THEY ASK FOR ...
THIS COURSE OF CONDUCT LEADS BOTH PARENT AND
CHILD SWIFTLY DOWN THE PATH OF MISERY.'

A well-mannered child is a delight to behold and may be presented in public, at tea parties and such like without embarrassment or fear of contrary conduct. Indeed, the behaviour of one's child is a decisive indicator of one's place within society. A mismanaged child is nothing but a regrettable stain upon the fabric of polite company and may be expected to achieve naught in life but the breaking of his poor mother's heart.

A mother, being the nearest and dearest to the infant, is singularly responsible for the proper advancement and refinement of its malleable mind. It is never too early to teach an infant the rules of obedience: even a babe in arms can recognise a smile of approval or a frown of

reproach! It is a mother's solemn duty towards the cultivation of a genteel society to instruct her child that at
particular times and in particular places it may *not* do
what, at other times and in other places, is perfectly
permissible. A mother *must* establish her ruling influence
and this can be achieved most effectively by withholding
or granting certain things which are greatly coveted by
the child. In this manner the mother's rule is most
forcibly felt.

Do not give in to feelings of excessive fondness nor
shower upon your child all that they ask for. There can be
no more effective mode of spoiling a child's character than
by inverting the natural order of things and placing the
reins firmly in the hands of the young usurper. This course
of conduct leads both parent and child swiftly down the
path of misery. There are some who would believe that no
harm can come of letting a mere babe have its own way.
This is an unfortunate misconception; indeed, if a babe is
of an age to express its wants by means of angered cries,
for example, then it is surely capable of learning the
precious habits of obedience.

Little children are possessed of a passionate and some-
what compulsive habit of seizing upon whatever object
they may desire. This habit should be checked with great
firmness as nurseries are full of dangers and articles of an
injurious nature such as hot coals, lighted candles and
kettles of scalding water. If a child persists in his attempt
to touch such forbidden articles, even after numerous

prohibitions, then a slight burn, bruise or scald may prove to be a merciful and memorable lesson. On these occasions, the infant should be given no sympathy, but made to understand that his injury is of his own making as he did not do as he was bidden.

Children should be taught to eat whatever is given to them, at whatever time it is offered. On no account should they be given scraps to eat between meals. If a child refuses his meal in a fit of passion, whether through disappointment or contrariness, then he should be removed from the table, sent from the room and the original nourishment offered at subsequent mealtimes until it is entirely consumed. Indeed, the importance of table manners cannot be emphasised sufficiently and the following rules should be instilled in a child from the earliest age:

* Do not present yourself at the table unless your hands and face are clean and your hair neatly combed.
* Do not presume to find fault with any dish that is given you.
* Do not spit, cough or blow your nose at the table.
* Do not pick your teeth at the table unless your mouth is shielded by a napkin.
* Take what you are served, whether it be to your taste or not. Eccentricity in regard to nourishment should be avoided at all times.

* Use your napkin habitually.

* Do not curl your feet under the table.

* Do not wear gloves at the table.

* Punctuality is requisite.

* Ladies are to sit before gentlemen.

* Do not pick up your knife and fork until you have been served.

* Eat slowly to ensure good health, greater wealth and an excess of happiness.

The manner in which a child presents itself in company is evidence to the success of its upbringing. Teach your child the following rules, forcibly and mercilessly:

* When invited into the company of your betters, do not sit or speak unless bidden.

* Do not put your hand to any part of your body not ordinarily discovered.

* Do not stand wriggling your person, but keep upright and steady.

* Do not sing or hum, or murmur to yourself.

* Do not look wilfully or boldly into the faces of your betters.

* Do not whisper.

* Do not stand with hands in pockets, scratch your head

or wink your eyes. Stand firm, looking straight ahead, with your hands folded neatly behind you.

Every child is born selfish, but it is by imparting the correct rules of obedience and conduct from the earliest moments of their lives that you can ensure their well-managed behaviour reflects most favourably upon you, their mother.

❧

BASED ON AN EXTRACT FROM *THE SCHOOL OF GOOD MANNERS* BY NATHANIEL PATTEN, 1787, AND OTHER EIGHTEENTH CENTURY SOURCES ON THE MANNER OF RAISING CHILDREN

How to Write an Encrypted Letter

'IF YOU EMBARK UPON EXCHANGING LETTERS OF LOVE
DURING COURTSHIP, SEE TO IT THAT YOU PAY CAREFUL
HEED TO ANY PROMISES YOU MAKE THEREIN ... YOU MAY
FIND YOURSELF HAVING MADE PROMISES THAT LATER, AS A
WIFE, YOU WOULD BE LOATH INDEED TO FULFIL.'

A respectable lady will long have acknowledged the inestimable importance of crafting a beautiful letter. She is judged in all respects by her correspondences: in her choice of stationery, the scented oils with which she mixes her ink, the satin ribbons or pressed flowers with which she adorns the borders, and in the exquisite finery of her grammar and penmanship. She is much practised at the close scrutiny of her syntax; pausing with every word to ascertain whether it is the very best that she can conjure. It is in the perfection of the letter's construction that a lover will be persuaded of the perfection of a lady's virtue.

If you embark upon exchanging letters of love during

courtship, see to it that you pay careful heed to any promises you make therein; a lover's letter can so often be the source of wearisome empty flattery and insincere assurances. If you are guilty of such misdemeanours, you may find yourself having made promises that later, as a wife, you would be loath indeed to fulfil. What you commit to paper must be guarded and dignified, no matter how the throes of love may persuade you otherwise.

Once married, your letters of love may take on a different hue. The love between a man and his wife can be most effectively celebrated in letter form, whenever business occasions their separation. Whilst it is nevertheless important that a wife maintain her dignity, much may be conveyed in a *lightly* encrypted fashion. 'Coffers' may be 'sapped' and tributes made to a husband's 'copious love' with which one longs to be 'brimming full'.

You may have occasion to find yourself in the sensitive position of having to give out a message of some delicacy to a trusted friend or relation. Where there is any chance that your letters may be intercepted and read by the very person whom it would be most disadvantageous to so do, may we advise the following encrypted contrivance: that of *reading between the lines.* Consider the following excerpt from a wife's very frank letter to her sister:

It is an unburdening of my heart, in truth,
to be able to tell you of the utter

misery in which I now pass my days.
My husband must surely be the most
insufferable, cantankerous, and unsightly
tyrant, whose dictum it is to subdue and suppress his
wife…

Naturally, in such a case no wife can contemplate being uncovered in such an unburdening by her husband. If, on the contrary, such a husband was to intercept a seemingly flattering letter, it may so impress upon him the ladylike qualities of his wife that he may be moved to a more gentle approach toward her. Thus, let the letter she sends out to her dearest sister read thus:

It is an unburdening of my heart, in truth,

to read of your continuing good health, dearest sister, and

to be able to tell you of the utter

good fortune I feel in finding myself in a state so far removed from

misery in which I now pass my days.

I count myself the luckiest wife in England!

My husband must surely be the most

estimable model for all those men who would otherwise become

insufferable, cantankerous and unsightly.

He should take such men and teach them the error of their ways, that they be not a

tyrant, whose dictum it is to subdue and suppress his wife…

No sister may fail to appreciate that the tone of such a letter bears little correspondence to her knowledge of her brother-in-law in reality (whereas a man will most likely be deaf, dumb and blinded to all the letter's subtleties). In such a case, a lady would, by all means, be moved to *read between the lines*, and in this way come to learn of the realities of her sister's predicament.

It is fair to say that a lady of refinement must needs fill her days with lightweight occupations, such as the writing of letters. But as every lady (and mercifully few gentlemen) will recognise, there is nothing at all lightweight in the ingenious construction of some of the most excellent examples of a lady's correspondence, despite all initial impressions to the contrary.

Inspired by original advice in assorted Victorian letter-writing manuals

How to Avoid the Paroxysms of Sleep

'IN HER GROANS AND MOANS MAY BE DETECTED HER
SENSATION THAT A SINGULAR LOAD LIES OPPRESSING HER
ABOUT THE BREAST; OTHER TIMES HER TOSSING AND
THRASHING BELIE HER VAIN ATTEMPTS AT FLEEING
SOME UNKNOWN ENEMY.'

Nothing can be so distressing as to see the once-blooming countenance of youth made old prematurely! Sadly, this is so often the consequence of a ravaging of sleep that is brought about by the paroxysm of the nightmare. Sleep is requisite for the good health of mind and body: too little will dull spirits and render frantic the nerves.

Sound sleep is essential in the prevention of the paroxysm, and sound sleep can never be sought out in a bed that is damp! Never reserve a bed solely for visitors, but see that it is kept in regular use by your servants, to be cast out when called upon for use by guests. Nothing is as injurious to the health and to sleep as a damp bed, for it blocks the perspiration. See, too, that your servants do not practise that accursed custom of dampening used sheets whilst still on the mattress, whereupon they are pressed with hot irons to save having to wash them. Putting linen upon a mattress that has been 'revived' (and, most sinisterly, *left dampened*) in such a way will bring about the death of the sleeper as surely as a gun shot!

One suffering from the nightmare should never be permitted to sleep alone. An onlooker is necessary that sleep be interrupted before the paroxysm is allowed to make firm its hold. The paroxysm is evident to the onlooker in the somnolent thrashings and muffled mutterings of the sleeper. Sometimes, in her groans and moans, may be detected her sensation that a singular load lies oppressing her about the breast; other times her tossing and thrashing belie her vain attempts at fleeing some unknown enemy. If the onlooker should be witness to a spasm or jerk of great force, such as would seem to fling her from her bed, it is evidence of the nightmare having tossed the sufferer over an abyss, or the like. In any event, it falls upon the onlooker to awaken the sufferer *at once*. Should a paroxysm take hold one night, it will grow in strength so that it may recur the next. An habitual paroxysm will be all the greater in potency and therefore all the more challenging to throw off.

It has been understood that the nightmare has as its cause an excess of blood about the brain, causing inertia of the cerebral fluids, so that blood would needs be drawn from the temples. Indeed, in persistent cases this may be so. However, in most instances, a preventative measure will be wholly successful. A look to the axiom, 'Light suppers cause sound sleep!' is most surely called for: the light diet and good digestion of the sufferer may suffice to alleviate the disease.

Poor digestion and a nervous disposition at the retiring hour are most often at fault. See that you do not indulge in the current trend among some circles for a supper as late as ten or eleven o'clock in the evening. Such foolhardiness is a formal invitation to the paroxysm! See that any grief or concerns that trouble you during the day are readily cast aside upon retiring, lest they be translated into nightmare in your sleep. Wind is another common cause, so that flatulent foods should be avoided during the evening. Peppermint water, or brandy, taken after eating will relieve turgid wind sufficiently to prevent trouble.

Another fault may be the passing of a restless and wakeful night, a fashion with a growing following, calling themselves 'night-watchers', apt to cast their gaze aloft to the night skies to indulge their love of all things celestial. This is *certain* to result in paroxysm the following night as sleep, long overdue, will be too deep. Avoid the practice at all costs!

If the sufferer of the paroxysm be young in years, a most heartily recommended remedy is the purging of bloods to assist with her good digestion. The bloods are plentiful in youth, and this can be detrimental to the brain. Thereafter see that the diet is plain and of small proportions: excess and indulgence at the last meal is as sure to result in paroxysm in children as it is in the mature.

BASED ON THE MEDICAL ADVICE IN EIGHTEENTH CENTURY MEDICAL MANUALS, SUCH AS DR W. BUCHAN'S *DOMESTIC MEDICINE*, 1785

How to Dress for and Take Pleasure from the Opera

'IT IS ILL BRED FOR A LADY TO BE SEEN STARING AROUND
THE HOUSE WITH HER OPERA GLASSES; A MODEST DIGNITY
IS NEVER MORE BEFITTING THAN WHEN PRACTISED IN A
PUBLIC PLACE.'

It is imperative that a lady be seen at the opera at least
once a week. To absent oneself for too long a period will
encourage scurrilous rumours to be sent whispering
between the aisles and in and out of the boxes. On occasion it may seem tiresome to pay tribute to performers of
questionable ability, but it is *your* performance and appearance, and that of the ladies in your set, that will render the
night most 'brilliant!'

You must never wear anything less than the most sumptuous of gowns, and your jewellery for the evening should
be splendid in its cut and brilliance, and displayed to all
advantage. Nothing less than a perfectly executed toilet
will do; every pair of glasses in the house will be pointed

in your direction. A lady would do well to remember that her opera gloves are the most essential and elegant ingredient of her costume. The best of opera gloves are fashioned from the softest and most exquisite of kidskin, and should be treated with the utmost care. The smaller your hands and the longer and tighter your gloves, then the more divine and entrancing a figure you will present. It is necessary that your gloves be a size too small to do most justice to the slenderness of your arms. Never attempt to don your gloves in public; it is a task best left to the privacy of your boudoir as it can prove arduous and time consuming to roll on a particularly tight-fitting and delicate glove.

An accomplished lady will always work her hand into the glove from the wrist and then gradually smooth the remainder up her arm. One should never pull a glove on from the top. The longest of opera gloves will have 21 buttons and will require powdering to ease on to your arms and a button hook to fasten. A lady well-schooled in the sensibilities of gentlemen may afford this difficult but particular pleasure to an enthusiastic escort. Have no doubt he will relive the experience for many nights to come!

An evening at the opera is the only occasion, excepting maybe a formal religious ceremony, where attention to correct manners and formal behaviour is so exacting. The very beat of your heart will be displayed to all and must prove virtuous and dignified in its rhythm! Your host for the night must be rigorous in his duties; any ignorance of etiquette will be noted (and you can be sure will increase four-fold in the telling), and will prove most detrimental to your own character. The gentleman should be in full dress: tail coat, white waistcoat, white tie and white gloves. He should wear his high hat at all times; only gentlemen unable to secure a box may wear collapsible hats as viewing is often obscured in the lower seats.

On arriving at the Opera House, your host will relieve you of your wrap and escort you through the foyer to your box for the evening. He will hold back the drapes to allow you and any other ladies in your party to enter. The most distinguished lady present will be accorded the corner seat nearest to the stage. Your host must never seat himself in the front row of a box even though there may be room available. He should see to it that the drapes are closed tight behind, permitting no light to obscure your view of the audience.

It is ill bred for a lady to be seen staring around the house with her opera glasses; a modest dignity is never more befitting than when practised in a public place. However, once the performance is under way, a lady, well-versed in discretion, may glean all she wishes to know while apparently giving her full concentration to the stage. The opera glass is a frisky instrument and you would do well to employ it judiciously.

Whilst promenading in the foyer between acts, you may nod at acquaintances or converse for no more than a minute or two. Do not speak of the 'opera', nor offer your opinions on the performance to those who are not habitual frequenters: your insights will be wasted upon them and, indeed, will draw their attention away from your dazzling costume. When the opera is ended you may show your appreciation with a gentle applause, but *never* exclaim, 'How lovely!' or, 'How exquisite!' These comments are left to those who are endowed with an underlying vulgarity.

Your host must wait with you in the lobby and see you and any other ladies safely into a carriage. If the evening has proved a success, the boxes being fully occupied and your head full of rich gossip to impart, you may feel inclined to offer him a ride; if however the evening was lacking in brilliance and fashionable personages, you are at liberty to thank your host most coldly and leave him to secure his own carriage home.

ADAPTED FROM ADVICE GIVEN IN *RULES OF ETIQUETTE AND HOME CULTURE* BY WALTER R. HOUGHTON ET AL., 1884

How to Go A-Foraging for Food about Your Estate

'MAY YOU REVEL IN YOUR GROANING FRUIT ORCHARDS, AND
MAY YOUR COOK BESTOW UPON YOUR GUESTS THE RUSTIC
GLEE OF PUDDINGS, JELLIES AND PIES! FOR WHAT MAN
THAT SITS REPLETE WITH A BELLY FULL OF APPLE PASTY
CAN HELP BUT WEAR A SMILE?'

There has of late emerged a tendency to shy away from the Whiggish obsession with the French cook. Our too-long love affair with the intolerable *cuisine* of that race has become indulgent and unpatriotic in the extreme, and the serving of meats cooked in gluey Frankish sauces, vulgar. It is fitting, then, that we now herald the return of truly *English* pleasures. May your meats be plain roasted and your fish swimming in nothing more veiling than butter! May you revel in your groaning fruit orchards, and may your cook bestow upon your guests the rustic glee of puddings, jellies and pies! For what man that sits replete with a belly full of apple pasty can help but wear a smile?

Firstly, see that your gardener is equipped with the latest

techniques for cultivating ever new varieties of orchard fruits. The addition of nut orchards, along with the likes of melon and cucumber, will lend a most welcome diversity to your table. It is not sufficient that your estate boasts an apple orchard; see that it boasts orchards of *assorted varieties* of apple, for it is in this that you are most likely to impress.

It is a most seemly pastime for a lady to look to supplement the cultivated fruits on her estate with a little foraging. Select an agreeable afternoon in early summer in which to walk abroad through your park, searching out locations where the woodland earth is at its most generous. Here, nestled quietly among the undergrowth, with mint green leaves and tiny berries of the reddest hue, are to be found the most delightful of bounties: the wild strawberry! Certainly, you may have your gardener cultivate plants, but there is little to compare with the private enchantment of happening upon sweet, wild fruit! Guard yourself against indulging in too many at the scene and see that a sufficient number make it into your basket that your cook may work her magic upon them.

Look out, too, for red, white and black currants, as they are all highly prized gems with which your cook may rustle up such delights as will liven up game, and add untold pleasure to pastries and puddings. Dewberries and blackberries, sloes and elderberries, are all most satisfactory late summer harvests, though be cautioned against the sampling of the elderberry fresh from the branch. It will only become palatable after cooking. Reject any berries growing on a plant that looks bruised or unwholesome: if the plant be not strong, the berries are unlikely to be at their best.

Even in the autumn months, a crisp morning's walk may be well rewarded if you happen upon a medlar tree bearing its browning, over-ripe fruits, full to bursting with their yielding, succulent flesh. In essence and form, the medlar will call to mind the pear that has been cooked down. Treat yourself to one straight from the branch: squeeze the fruit until it yields its superior stuffing, rejecting both the skin without and the stone within. But gather some into your basket to be transformed into the most delectable puddings.

All these wild fruits and berries, when preserved and combined with the fruits of your orchards, are most essential in the production of desserts that will charm the company at your table. Moreover, many are very versatile, being exquisite when candied, and highly beneficial when distilled into medicinal waters.

As your knowledge of the greatest catches upon your estate grows, it can be a most pleasing way to entertain your lady guests, and the perfect precursor to a picnic.

How to Go A-Foraging for Food about Your Estate

What can be more patriotic than a happy hour spent cele-
brating the fruits of Mother England, knowing that your
labours will soon come to grace your dining table to the
delight of your guests?

INSPIRED BY LATE EIGHTEENTH CENTURY HOUSEHOLD AND
RECIPE BOOKS, AND THE ARISTOCRATIC FASCINATION WITH
THE CULTIVATION OF FRUIT

How to Identify a Changeling Child

'THE HUMAN CHILD IS POSSESSED OF A FAR GREATER
BEAUTY AND INTELLIGENCE, THUS INCREASING QUALITY AND
STOCK WHEN INTRODUCED INTO A FAIRY CLAN.'

It is no small endeavour for a lady of tender nerves to be possessed the means to intelligently identify a changeling child; especially during the early days of motherhood when one would expect to be suffering under a delicate disposition.

It is most common for a changeling to be at first discovered by the mother who finds that her own dear and pretty child has been snatched from its cradle. In its place is laid a wizened and deformed fairy child, with thick head and staring eyes, who does nought but guzzle milk greedily and howl in a most inhuman fashion. That fairy folk should wish to exchange their own ill-tempered, *troll-like* young for a human child is no mystery. The human child is possessed of a far greater beauty and intelligence, thus increasing quality and stock when introduced into a fairy clan. It is a most distressing situation to find oneself in and although the child under suspicion may be in possession of one or more well-known changeling traits, this in itself can be no guarantee of its other-worldly identity.

There are a number of tell-tale signs which should alert a mother to the swapping of her child. Her offspring may grow uglier by the day and be possessed by a voracious appetite which shows no sign of being satisfied. The child may be in possession of unusual facial features or markings. He may have pointed ears or be stunted in growth, and although of less than usual intelligence, he will most certainly show cunning beyond his years. It is advisable to keep the child for several days, observing all the signs. Once sure you can no longer tolerate the usurper you must choose your course of action.

Many will advise you to mistreat the child by placing it in a hot oven, beating it with a switch until it screams, or bathing it in a solution of foxglove. Indeed, many advocate placing the suspected changeling in a shovel and holding him over an open fire. Those who profess to be experts in this matter state that a changeling child will howl out in pain, whilst a true human will remain silent. It is said that these acts of cruelty will force the hand of the fairy folk and ensure the return of the original child. These practices, however, are not to be recommended: they are vulgar and may leave your reputation open to criticism and ruin, should it be proven that the child is indeed innocent. There is also the matter of the mistreatment being replicated on the human child, should his fairy abductors witness the suffering of the changeling.

The commonsense way to identify a changeling is to make him laugh, or trick him into an utterance of surprise. The means employed to bring about this reaction is to cook a family meal in an eggshell. This should be done in full sight of the interloper and should bring about his laughter or cause him to exclaim, 'I have seen the acorn before the oak, but I never saw the likes of this!' Once exposed, the fairy folk have no choice but to take the changeling child back from whence he came and restore your own child to his natural place.

It is wise to indulge in preventative practices in order to lessen the risk of fairy exchange. All women who have recently been delivered should not give in to sleep until a trusted nurse is watching over the newborn; a steel item such as a pair of scissors or a knife laid upon the cradle will help ward off unwanted visitors. If no such method brings about a fortunate outcome, and you have no ready access to a learned sorcerer, then the best you can do is to endeavour to raise the creature as if it were your own beloved child.

BASED ON COMMON BELIEFS FROM THE MIDDLE AGES
THROUGH TO THE EIGHTEENTH CENTURY

How to Play Parlour Games

'WHEN THERE IS A GAY PARTY GATHERED TOGETHER IN
THE PARLOUR THEN MANY WILL MAKE KNOWN THEIR
DESIRE FOR MERRY GAMES.'

Even the most industrious and demure of ladies will find themselves ready, at times, for fun and frolic of the household kind. There can be no greater delight, during the long dark evenings of winter and early springtime, than to participate in the innocent amusements of youth. When there is a gay party gathered together in the parlour then many will make known their desire for merry games. There is any number of these entertainments, but we will lay out before you a few of our very favourites.

Shadows: This game causes much amusement in a happy gathering. It consists of the detection of individuals by their shadows alone; every person being at liberty to disguise their outline as much as is practicable. A white cloth should be suspended on one side of the room and a person elected as guesser. This guesser is to sit facing the cloth with a lamp or candle alight at a distance behind him. The remaining party takes turns to pass before the lamp and behind the guesser thus throwing a strong shadow upon the cloth. They must not pass by in their natural attitude but must contrive to change their outline as much as possible by means of hunching, bending of limbs or changing coats and hoods. Whoever is correctly detected then takes the place of the guesser.

The Ball of Wool: The company should be seated around a table from which the cloth has been removed. A small length of wool is rolled into a ball and placed in the centre of the table. The company then commences to blow upon the ball, each endeavouring to steer it away from his own direction. All should aim to blow it off the table so the person by whose right side it falls may pay a forfeit. The game affords much mirth when looking upon the fervent exertions and swollen cheeks of the players!

The Courtiers: One of the party should be selected to play King or Queen and the rest made to sit around the sides of the room. The Monarch should proceed to making any movement of his choosing and the assembled 'courtiers' should follow suit. The Monarch may choose to blow his nose, to yawn or to sneeze, and if any of the courtiers do not imitate this movement with exacting decorum or indeed if they fall to laughter or smiles, then they must pay a forfeit.

The Dumb Orator: A merry distraction enacted by two members of the party for the delight of the remainder. A member of the party possessed with eloquent and musical diction should stand perfectly motionless whilst reciting a chosen speech or piece of writing. The other person chosen should stand by his side and remain utterly silent while all the time gesticulating wildly according to the emotions brought about by the reading. The more closely the actions follow the reading and the more ridiculous the motions, then the greater will be the hilarity afforded.

Forfeits: Many games require the losers to pay a forfeit, indeed 'crying the forfeits' is often the most gratifying part of an evening's entertainment. Each person allotted a forfeit must pass some personal trinket or article into the hands of one appointed as the collector. The article could be a handkerchief, a hair decoration or a comb. The collector is blindfolded and must pick one of the articles, then declare, 'Here is a thing, a very pretty thing. What shall be done to the owner of this thing?'

An appropriate task is then declared. A gentleman, for instance, may be called upon to kiss each lady in the room. For this he is blindfolded and the company may change their positions often so he may find himself kissing the *back* of a lady's head, or indeed attempting to kiss one of his own gender! A gentleman may also be required to 'Make a Grecian Statue'. This calls for him to stand upon a chair and position his limbs in a way chosen by the company to most resemble an elegant Grecian statue and to remain in said position for as long as the company so desires.

A lady's forfeit may require her to recite a proverb

backwards or to imitate any animal that may be named. If this forfeit happens to fall upon a lady who from age or any other unfortunate disposition should be excused from such a performance, then a man is named as the chosen animal and a bow from him deemed sufficient.

All of these entertainments should be conducted in a manner of harmless frivolity, avoiding boisterous and unseemly behaviour in which a sensitive mind could find cause for offence. Those who enter into any frivolous diversion should be prepared to give as much amusement as they themselves would wish to receive.

ADAPTED FROM ORIGINAL ARTICLES ON THE SUBJECT OF HOUSEHOLD AMUSEMENTS FROM *CASSELL'S HOUSEHOLD GUIDE*, C.1880S

How to Dress Your Hair

'PARTING THE HAIR ONLY SLIGHTLY TO ONE SIDE WILL
DECREASE YOUR AGE BY AS MUCH AS FIVE YEARS.
PRECIOUS ADVICE INDEED!'

The hair is a wondrous ornament which Mother Nature has seen fit to bestow in plenitude upon the fairer sex. Ladies of true beauty are blessed with tresses of the utmost fineness and brilliance (fair-coloured hair being the most becoming as all beguiling women throughout history have found to their advantage). Those unfortunates whose crowning glory is less than splendid, whose hair is lustreless, thin or coarse (or indeed as black as Newgate Knockers), need not despair altogether. With intelligent efforts many faults may be diminished and whatever little beauty there is can always be improved upon.

Whatever the colour of hair given you at birth, and however alluring a head of fair hair would seem, it is wise that one should work with the hue that Nature intended as this will best frame your face and be most becoming to your own colouring. There are some who would dye their hair a deep mahogany, and although they may use the most scientific methods available, be assured the results are no less than hideous. Those who are fair by *nature* may, however, enhance their fairness with the use of oxidised water with no detriment to *their* beauty.

Many women lack the courage to allow their hair to grow silver with age and endanger their health by the use of lead concoctions to disguise the ravages of time. It is far more becoming and dignified to accept the whitening of hair; indeed, many an elderly lady's face has improved and softened once youth has flown. Many ladies of advanced years would be well advised to cover their heads with a lace mantilla as the shadows thrown by the patterns of the lace do much to conceal the disheartening effects of time. An elderly lady displaying a bare head can be a frightful sight. Powdering the hair is also to be discouraged as it hardens the features and diminishes any natural charm.

It is as well to keep the hair and scalp clean, and this can be done admirably with a solution of salt and rainwater. A teacup of salt should be added to a quart of rainwater and left to stand for 12 hours. This decoction can then be rubbed into the hair and scalp, and rinsed off well. It is in the final dressing of the hair that a lady can most enhance her beauty but it does not follow that the most fashionable style of the moment will suit the character of every face.

Indeed, many a lady has found herself rendered ugly merely by adopting a *seemingly* popular design.

It is wise to first consider the features and structure of the figure in order to array the hair in the most becoming manner. If a lady is petite and fine boned, a large arrangement of hair will sit ridiculously. If possessed of overlarge features, in particular a high forehead, then scraping the hair back, *à la chinoise*, will have a most disastrous effect. An eccentric coiffure, embellished by false hair, is best avoided by ladies of refinement lest they be mistaken for ladies of less illustrious character.

The simple art of parting the hair can have a dramatic effect upon appearance. A parting engineered too far to one side will bestow a masculine countenance upon even the most feminine and delicate of wearers. However, parting the hair only slightly to one side will decrease your age by as much as five years. Precious advice indeed!

Although the wearing of false fringes does away with the disastrous crisping effects brought about by frequent use of hot irons to curl the short hairs around the forehead, these hairpieces themselves can be fraught with danger. Be aware that many false fringes, despite being purified, can communicate dreadful skin diseases to the wearer. It is never instantly obvious whether the hair has been procured from a living or dead person (although it is said that hair from deceased bodies can only be curled or frizzed with great difficulty).

Finally, the method of dressing the hair should be

altered frequently so as to avoid the thinning that will occur if hair is forever pulled in the same direction. It is no bad practice to surprise and delight your admirers as often as you are able!

BASED ON ETIQUETTE AND ADVICE MANUALS OF THE NINETEENTH CENTURY

How to Manage Your Servants with Mistrust and Misgiving

'THE SERVANT IS A SINGULAR BRUTE WHO WILL CONNIVE TO TAKE THE PATH OF LEAST RESISTANCE IN ALL THINGS. DESPITE THEIR LACK OF BREEDING OR WIT, THEY HAVE CONTRIVED TO ADAPT EVERY SITUATION TO THEIR OWN PECULIAR ADVANTAGE.'

There can be little that compares to the irksome weariness of troublesome servants. How many gentlewomen bemoan the intolerable insolence with which their housekeepers perform their duties, and perform them to a less than satisfactory standard? Alas, considerable is the cross that a wife is expected to bear when she undertakes to run a household of staff. How much greater the burden carried by the lady that cannot set aside her virtuous nature and Christian doctrine, for then will she mistakenly perceive all those in the employ of her husband to be of *sound character*.

This could not be further from the truth! The servant is

a singular brute who will connive to take the path of least resistance in all things. Despite their lack of breeding or wit, they have contrived to adapt every situation to their own peculiar advantage. Approach all your dealings with this in mind: never permit yourself the indulgence of placing your trust in any servant, and you will thereby arm yourself with the surest method of managing them efficaciously. In certain respects, we feel it is our duty to enlighten gentle ladies in the erroneous ways of their household staff so that you may be forearmed and fore-warned in the same circumstances.

Most arduous to a lady is the habit of the servant to resist any matter that is aside from that for which they are strictly in your employ. For instance, if the chambermaid be instructed to soak a single petticoat, the scullery maid being absent, she may be relied upon to reply that she does not have the skill with which such a task may adequately be carried out. Hence your petticoat remains sullied.

When occasion arises (and arise it surely will) to chide a servant, this must be done with the most resolute of sensibilities. No matter how brazen the fault, a servant so chastised is wont to give out an air of such impudence that, if unguarded, may persuade you to perceive that it is *they,* not you, who are the injured person. Furthermore, if you are given to reprimand him in the company of others, ensure that nonesoever see fit to interject in support of the wretch. For, in this instance, the seed may be sown in his mind that as you are wrong to chide him in this respect, so you will be in all others henceforth. In such a way will be transmitted to all below-stairs that you are mistaken in your reprimands.

Servants may be remunerated for their allegiance to you and your husband, but in truth it is to their fellow servants that they are most tied. This will induce the most intolerable effects on the occasion of any wrong-doing having been carried out by an unknown person. You may be sure to be presented with the family parrot, monkey or lap-dog as the culprit before they will admit that one of their own is at fault. The only exception being if the chance arises whereby they may allocate blame on your most valued and best-loved servant, at which chance they will leap with frequent interval. This will have a bearing in particular should you be informed that one of their number is absent due to 'ill health'. Any lady would, without hesitation, see that such an invalid servant would be provided with every comfort with which to speed their recovery. Guard yourself, therefore, whenever such apparent incapacities occur the morning after an evening's junket: an excess of ale and a long evening ill-spent in idle tattle is no cause for shirking and must be rewarded with your cudgelling, not your kindness.

Finally, your servants are sure to fulfil any task as indolently as they are able. Any errand worth 30 minutes or less of their time is sure to last several hours, and always with good cause. A visit to some uncle's death bed, or a soaking with some nastiness cast up from under the wheels of a carriage, or an unfortunate encounter of the foot with a sharp stone in the track; or, worse still, a fruit-less search in some three dozen taverns for your shillings in his guard, 'filched' by one who was, 'known to inhabit such a place' – whatever the excuse, be not tempted to respond favourably; it will always be a ruse.

If a lady manages her servants with a suspicious sensi-bility at all times, she may be sure to outwit them in most things so as to preserve her own, and her household's, well-being.

INSPIRED BY AND ADAPTED FROM *DIRECTIONS TO SERVANTS* BY JONATHAN SWIFT, 1739 (REPRINTED BY HESPERUS PRESS, 2003)

How to Conduct Yourself at a Ball

'A WELL-BRED GENTLEMAN WILL NEVER ASK A LADY TO
HONOUR HIM IN A DANCE WITHOUT PROPER INTRODUCTION.
IF SUCH AN IMPOLITENESS IS PUT TO YOU THEN YOU
SHOULD POSITIVELY REFUSE THE GENTLEMAN ... AND
MAKE KNOWN YOUR DISPLEASURE.'

The ballroom is a place where fine manners and courtesies should be observed to the highest degree. There can be nothing more delightful (or indeed preferred!) than an evening of dancing with a succession of well-bred and honourable partners.

A ball is an occasion for a lady of taste and refinement to wear her grandest and most fanciful attire. All your finest trimmings of lace, ribbons and flowers may be made use of in a creative and elaborate fashion. Gay-coloured dresses of the finest silks and gauzes should be matched to slippers of satin. We would urge you to forego the addition of a train, for although they appear elegant and costly, they are considered most impolite as they have a habit of getting under the feet of other dancers and gathering tears from the not-so nimble-footed.

White kid gloves are an indispensable addition to your toilet, as is a fine, lace-trimmed handkerchief and an eye-catching fan. It is to your advantage to carry with you a spare pair of gloves, should you happen to soil your original when partaking of refreshments. It would be mortifying indeed to offer a soiled hand to a handsome and most admired partner!

Married ladies may be accompanied to a ball by their husbands, but they are on no account to dance more than the first set together. It is most unseemly for a married couple to pay one another such attentions. Unmarried ladies must be accompanied by a chaperone; either a family friend or their own mother. It would be most scandalous for any lady, married or otherwise, to leave the ballroom and venture into an adjoining room without her husband or chaperone to accompany her.

You need not be punctual to a ball; indeed, punctuality speaks of ill-bred enthusiasm and a person unaccustomed to such pleasures. To arrive after others is most gratifying; the hours spent perfecting your toilet will therefore not go unnoticed, but will be commented on by all who witness your late entrance. Upon arrival, all ladies will be presented with a dance card on which to note the forthcoming evening's engagements. A lady of ingenuity will not allow her card to be filled too hastily lest she give herself cause for regret should a particularly admired gentleman friend happen to arrive late on in the evening. It should be noted that the last dance before supper is of particular interest as the gentleman who partners you in this instance will also escort you into supper.

Be certain that you have completed your toilet before entering the ballroom. It is considerably indecorous to be seen drawing on your gloves or adjusting your hair. These arrangements should be seen to in the dressing-room which your generous host will have made available to you.

A well-bred gentleman will never ask a lady to honour him in a dance without proper introduction. If such an impoliteness is put to you then you should positively refuse the gentleman (if he still deserves to be called thus!) and make known your displeasure. You may not refuse a gentleman a dance, however, once he has been formally introduced as he will be most insulted. A reasonable excuse must be offered so as not to harm his good intentions: a fit of the vapours or a sudden flush of heat may serve to excuse you.

Once engaged in dancing, a lady must endeavour to always wear a pleasant countenance whomsoever her partner may be. To engage in incessant talk will occasion unpleasant remarks and whispering in a partner's ear is the most scandalous of behaviours! If you are unfortunate enough to be partnered with an unpractised dancer who continually errs in his dance steps and draws the amused attentions of other dancers your way, then you may apprise him of his errors in a light-hearted manner, contriving to avoid the air of a teacher. If a falling should occur then be assured it will *always* be the man's fault as ladies are naturally graceful in their movements. The gentleman who embarrasses you in such an abominable manner should afford himself a number of dancing lessons before accepting any future invitations. Indeed, it is questionable whether the said gentleman should have been present at all!

It is considered ill-mannered to leave a ball directly after supper, but nor should you be the last to leave. A lady intent on prolonging her pleasure errs on the side of vulgarity. A quiet and unobtrusive retirement is most decorous.

ADAPTED FROM *BALLROOM ETIQUETTE FROM THE UNIVERSAL DANCING MASTER* BY LUCIEN O. CARPENTER, 1880, AND OTHER ETIQUETTE MANUALS

How to Mourn with Decorum

'YOUR DARLING HUSBAND'S BODY SHOULD BE LAID OUT
IN THE PARLOUR FOR THREE DAYS OR SO BEFORE THE
FUNERAL. A CLOSE WATCH MUST BE KEPT AT ALL TIMES
TO WARD OFF THE RATS WHICH WILL SURELY BE
ATTRACTED TO THE POOR SOUL'S REMAINS.'

When a beloved husband departs from this world and
your heart feels as if it will never heal, take comfort
from your station in life, your wealth and respectability.
A lady must *always* grieve correctly. From the very
instant your dear husband exhales his dying breath, be
assured you will have not one moment to dwell upon
your despair. As a good and faithful wife you must see to
it that all the necessary arrangements are put into place
to ensure your family and acquaintances are apprised of
the *measure* of your heartache.

Your darling husband's body should be laid out in the
parlour for three days or so before the funeral. A close
watch must be kept at all times to ward off the rats
which will surely be attracted to the poor soul's remains.

During this period you may not receive any callers offering their condolences, but may use the time wisely to prepare the entire household. The drapes should be drawn, the mirrors covered, and all the clocks halted. Indeed, Time itself should respect the passing of the head of the house. Your staff should attire themselves in black work dresses, caps and gloves. All paper used for correspondence should be reprinted with black edging and your calling cards the same (you may narrow the width of the black edging as mourning time passes). You must put aside all thoughts of pretty colours and fanciful ribbons as you don your widow's weeds and prepare yourself for Deep Mourning.

For a full year and a day after the departure of your husband you must wear a black crêpe dress and a weeping veil (that hideous banner of woe that fashion doth dictate!). The wearing of a dull and monotonous colour will show the world that the light has gone out of your life. You must not step outside of your home without the full black attire and only when you feel ready to bestow your presence upon society once more should you send cards to all friends and relatives. Your activities during this year will be restricted to attending church services and receiving visitors. No caller should offend your eye or insult your grief by the wearing of a bright colour.

You may find your crêpe costume troublesome, as the material is most disagreeable and tends to shrivel in the rain, and the veil is most restrictive to one's breathing. Bear all discomfort with grace, however, and you will earn admiration for your devotion to your dearly departed.

After a year and a day of grieving you may now enter Second Mourning. This period will last for nine months and you are permitted now to lift your veil and wear it on the back of your head. A small amount of ornamentation is acceptable and you may wish to wear discreet pieces of jet jewellery. A most delightful fashion is to have a lock of your beloved's hair woven into an intricate design and made use of in a brooch or necklace. A most loving way to keep him close to you!

After nine months you may enter into Half Mourning and do away with your veil altogether, although a quiet black hat would do you well. You may vary the colour of your costume now and introduce some greys or the subtlest of violets and mauves. A little trimming can be added to skirts and all manner of jewellery be reintroduced. After three months a gradual easing into colour is acceptable, although you may have enjoyed the respect afforded to a decorous widow and choose to continue to wear your mourning costume until an offer of marriage comes your way.

Not all relatives need be mourned in this fashion. Indeed, parents and children need only be mourned for a year; grandparents, brothers and sisters for six months. Aunts and uncles may be mourned for six weeks and first cousins for a period of four weeks.

How to Mourn with Decorum

The most solemn of all duties is that which we must perform for the dead. It is becoming in a lady to show in every possible way her deep sympathy and grief on the saddest of all occasions.

ADAPTED FROM 'MOURNING AND FUNERAL USAGES', *HARPERS BAZAAR*, 17 APRIL 1886

How to Abstain from Rendering Oneself Aloft Like a Witch

'THE GOOD GOVERNMENT OF OUR NATION HAS DECREED THAT WHILST WITCHCRAFT IS TO BE SOUGHT OUT AND DESTROYED BY DEATH, THE PRACTICE OF FLYING IS NOT, IN ITSELF, OBJECTIONABLE.'

God and England abhor the witch, and let no gentle-woman dispute His law. But the good government of our nation has decreed that whilst witchcraft is to be sought out and destroyed by death, the practice of flying is not, in itself, objectionable. This notwithstanding, assuredly no lady of breeding would condescend to such a base and unnatural activity.

The testimonies of witches across our land have given voice to a most heinous practice. By use of a magick salve, a treacherous hag can uncover the means with which to render herself aloft, flying through the air atop a broomstick, so as to attend her devilish Sabbat. Such ointments have been concocted and tested by physicians of some repute, using the receipts given out by these witches at the torturer's hand. The resulting ointment has been used upon certain individuals and thereafter carefully observed.

It is just conceivable that such an ointment or salve, with which the witch achieves her flight, could come into contact with a lady of decorum. Without prior knowledge, such a lady would not be sufficiently equipped as to avoid the unction, so as to prevent the magick flight from occurring. This being an intolerable circumstance, we herein lay before you the method by which such an ointment may be constructed, and the consequences of its application. In such a way may you be ever assured of protection.

That witches are known to fly is of no contention; any who have walked abroad under a full moon will have seen them leaping into the air amid fields of wheat. Many have borne witness to the anointing of their broomstick, in order to assist in both the application of the salve, and to equip the resultant flight. Sitting astride the broom, they thereafter hurtle and canter about, all the time clenching the broom against their unclothed gentlest parts.

This most mysterious salve can be detected first by its dark green hue and odious scent. Its most monstrous form, and that most strongly pertaining to witchery, is said to be derived from the distillations gathered from a red-headed Catholic, left hanging following his expiry at the hands of serpents or other venomous creatures. Such liquid thus culled is then mixed with the bodily grease of a corpulent hanged man, the innards of a child and whatever venom first brought about the death of the Catholic.

However, let it be known that a less repellent method of producing said salve is to combine pork fat (a substitution for that of the hanged man, or the child) with hemlock, the dried, crushed berries of the deadly nightshade, the boiled, black fungus that can be found growing on millet, and the milk of a toad mixed with urine and water. In such a way could a person contrive to construct a flying ointment without the use of magick or, indeed, of witchcraft. (Moreover, it may be said that this receipt contrives to do nothing greater than combine various ingredients of Nature; a gentle lady may *happen* upon a combination of these ingredients without so much as a whisper of anything more than a simple *botanical* fascination.)

The ointment, when applied to the delicate, hirsute areas of a lady's person, will rapidly work its way into the blood, creating first a quickening of the heart, then inducing a false sleep. It is now that the flight will occur, along with experiences of an intimate nature, such as would never be experienced in life by a lady of delicate persuasion. Indeed, it is said that on the continent a physician undertook to test out the green salve upon the wife of an executioner (it being neither right nor fitting to employ the services of a gentlewoman). Her words upon waking stand as a caution to all: she informed her husband that not only had she taken flight during her sleep, but furthermore she no longer had the need for him as she had been satiated by another and was now quite replete. Thus by such a means had he been rendered a cuckold! (And by one who did not reek of the gallows, no doubt.) Mark you, we have heard on good authority that a smile of so rapacious a hue was fixed upon her countenance that it caused the goodly physician to look away and blush.

INSPIRED BY THE TORTURED 'CONFESSIONS' OF SIXTEENTH CENTURY EUROPEAN WOMEN ACCUSED OF WITCHERY AND BY THE WORK OF M. J. HARNER ON 'THE ROLE OF HALLUCINOGENIC PLANTS IN EUROPEAN WITCHCRAFT', 1973

Epilogue

We hereby lay down our weary pens, having imparted to you but a fragment of the wisdom at our disposal. We have endeavoured to present the collected wit of generations of ladies. Our intention has been to urge that all ladies of rank carry themselves with honour, paying as much respect to their dignity as they do to the lesser trivialities of their equipage. Beauty without restraint is no paradigm to which ladies of society should aspire! Renown for one's looks and toilet alone can be no substitute for a reputation for decorous living and delicate sensibilities. If we but reject all whim and extravagance as folly, we might, indeed, herald in a Golden Age.

'Tis true that many a fine lady wants for a fine learning, but 'tis a falsehood to presume that her wit is therefore beneath the *scope* of a gentleman's. Nature provides many a young woman with an unformed but ready mind. If we relish matters only more serious and ingenuous, our inconsequential world of tittle-tattle and scandal would be stifled for ever.

Epilogue

As you linger over the pages of this most useful and valuable work, abounding with instructions and encouragements, we would remind you that it was our intention to render the work *practical*, so as to have it a book to be *read*. Our aim was to instruct, not dazzle; to infuse the minds of untutored young ladies with the most correct of principles. We trust these pages have proved both delightful and edifying, and with confidence we declare that this dedicated volume will become your most intimate companion.

EPILOGUE INSPIRED, IN PART, BY THE WRITINGS OF MRS CRACKENTHORPE IN THE EIGHTEENTH CENTURY PERIODICAL, *THE FEMALE TATLER*